THE BEAUTIFUL UN-BECOMING

THE ULTIMATE GUIDE TO LIFE AFTER SPIRITUAL AWAKENING

LYNDSAY K.R. TOENSING

Cover Design: Jennifer Stimson

Editor: Cory Hott

Author's photo courtesy of: Elisa Eminger

"*The Beautiful Un-Becoming* is infused with a quality of light that gently, boldly, and penetratingly calls the soul on the path of awakening to fully embrace and cherish the journey – challenging though it may be. At once deceptively simple and rock-bottom deep, Lyndsay's own story, the stories of her clients, and the rich tool-chest she generously shares, provide an alluring nectar of inquiry, reflection, and action to support the awakening process. A wise and brilliant guide."

— ROBIN WINN, LMFT, HUMAN DESIGN COACH, FOUNDER OF UNDERSTANDING YOUR CLIENTS THROUGH HUMAN DESIGN TRAINING PROGRAM, AND BESTSELLING AUTHOR OF *UNDERSTANDING YOUR CLIENTS THROUGH HUMAN DESIGN*

"What a life saver this book is. In a time that can feel very isolating and ungrounding, *The Beautiful Un-Becoming* throws you a much-needed lifeline. Lyndsay lays out a clear, practical, and approachable game plan to help you navigate and make sense of the spiritual awakening process. Bravo."

— EVAN JONES, WHOLE PERSON
CERTIFIED COACH

"*The Beautiful Un-Becoming* is a loving and supportive companion and step by step guide for a journey of self-discovery. Through every delicious bite-size piece, you can feel Lyndsay's love and support as you morph into exactly who you are meant to be. What a gift."

— REBECCA SCHLITZ, LICENSED
MARRIAGE AND FAMILY THERAPIST

"I left *The Beautiful Un-Becoming* with less self-loathing and so much more self-love. I felt less alone in my spiritual journey, and more empowered to learn that what I am feeling is 'normal.' She makes you really look at what you are feeling inside and the reasons behind it, as well as gives you tools to help explore it. It's such an insightful book that breaks things down so anyone can understand it."

— KELLY LUITEN, MOTHER

"Lyndsay Toensing's new book, *The Beautiful Un-Becoming: The Ultimate Guide to Life after Spiritual Awakening,* is a precious gem. Lyndsay gives a raw and vulnerable account of her own struggles in life and awakening. The metaphor of the butterfly's metamorphosis beautifully demonstrates how we can awaken to a fulfilling spiritual life when we shed the literal and figurative shell of our past. Lyndsay shares her own metamorphosis that led her to create a spiritually rich life to show you a path to do the same.

This book is like having a down to earth conversation with Lyndsay, which makes it easy to read and understand for spiritual seekers of all levels. Embrace her recipe to 'follow what nourishes your soul', live it daily and you will becomes the person you were always were meant to be, as Lyndsay puts it so truthfully."

— DR. H.C. PETRA FRESE, INTUITIVE SCIENTIST, BCH, CI

"*The Beautiful Un-Becoming* is the perfect companion guide to your journey in becoming all that you were born to be. This book will fill your heart with hope, love, joy and the divine wisdom that comes from living a soul led life. Recommended reading for anyone on the spiritual path."

— BROOKE ALEXANDER, SPIRITUAL MENTOR, MASTER TRANSFORMATIONAL COACH, FOUNDER OF YOUR LEGACY PROJECT, AND CREATOR OF THE PATH METHOD™

"*The Beautiful Un-Becoming* is the perfect blend of guidance, insights, and support for those looking to live their most fulfilled life after spiritual awakening. A must read for those looking to feel understood and supported as they navigate a new way of life."

— ANGELA DODD, MBA, MS

"Stop what you're doing right now (run, don't walk), go purchase *The Beautiful Un-Becoming* and begin reading and journaling. If you've ever had a thought, no matter how fleeting, that there is more to life than what you're currently experiencing, then this guide is FOR you. This book/guide is 100% pure magic for anyone spiritually curious, in the midst of their spiritual awakening or just coming out of experiencing a universal smackdown because you've just been ignoring all the divine signs. Lyndsay so beautifully maps out what this process looks, feels and requires to come out on the other side the version of yourself that you were born to be: beautiful, perfect, divine and pure love."

— JENNIFER HONEY, INTUITIVE LIFE COACH AND HUMAN DESIGN SPECIALIST, REBELS 4 LOVE COACHING

"*The Beautiful Un-Becoming* comes from the author's heart. Lyndsay walks you through the whole process of spiritual awakening, through pain and struggles, to discovering joy, love, fulfillment and peace. And it's done with firsthand experience and knowledge, she gives you tools, practices and exercises to help you navigate through your awakening. Lyndsay's book lets you know that you are not alone on your journey.

She completely brings 'you' into her book. There were moments I was wondering if Lyndsay was speaking directly to me. One part really stuck out for me, she wrote: 'But it is through your greatest struggles that you will heal and becomes the beautiful, unique, strong creature that can take flight and create the life you never imagined possible.' I highly recommend this book to everyone."

— ALICIA PETSCHL, MOTHER

"I was hooked by the 1st paragraph of *The Beautiful Un-Becoming*. It feels as it was written for me, for right now, and my guides are dancing with excitement. Perfect cosmic alignment. Highly recommend if you are feeling stuck, however, know there is more. Trust Lyndsay's experiences and knowledge to help you thru this journey. Live your best life."

— KELLY CROCKER, ENTREPRENEUR

"Anyone who is beginning the journey, or somewhere in the middle of their spiritual awakening, knows how confusing, scary, and unnerving the process is. As I began to read the pages of *The Beautiful Un-Becoming*, I would find myself responding out loud as if I was having a discussion with a friend, looking for validation for what I was going through, asking questions, nodding, shouting, 'Yes.' You connect deeply with Lyndsay as she explains what's happening, what to expect, and why as she walks you through the process. You feel the love, grace, and gentleness that she truly gives to everyone she knows. You are put at ease. Beautifully written book for anyone who is on their spiritual awakening path."

— JESSICA OLSON, HUMAN RESOURCES MANAGER

"*The Beautiful Un-Becoming* is a must for anyone who is soul searching or who has contemplated 'a dark night of their soul.' For those of us who have reached crossroads in our lives and are hungry for more than just a 'physical' experience, this book will open your eyes to the power of awakening the soul. It is a clear, step-by-step guide to transform your life's journey, learning to let go of what can be seen and embrace what cannot be seen."

— JOSH HARLAN, CLINICAL ANALYST

CONTENTS

To my soul family – thank you for loving, supporting, and seeing me when I couldn't see myself.

AWAKE AND CONFUSED

"Two roads diverged in a wood, and I—I took the one less traveled by, and that has made all the difference."

— ROBERT FROST

Going through a spiritual awakening process can be one of the loneliest, most confusing, and challenging experiences of your life. Nothing makes sense anymore. You question everything you believed in for most of your life. You are trying to understand why you do the things you do and why you became the person you became. At the same time, you are beginning to see through the illusion of societal programming and conditioning that told you who to be and how to operate in the world. You don't have anyone to talk to because no one you know has been through this. The people, places, and things that once resonated with you no longer attract or inspire you. You know you can't go back to your old way of operating in the world, but you don't know how to move forward with your new beliefs and how you now want to show up in the world. Does that sound about right?

You are here because you have gone through a spiritual awakening -- no longer who you were but not yet who you were meant to be -- and you are looking for support adjusting to this new life. Please know you are not alone. Many others, including me, have been through this. This is an initiation to un-become who you were so that you can step into who you were always meant to be. Welcome, and thank you for trusting me to support you on this journey.

DISCLAIMER

At this point, I feel the need to give you my disclaimer. This book is not intended to provide nor replace professional medical or psychiatric treatment. Please seek professional care if you believe you may have a medical or psychiatric condition.

It is incredibly important to reach out to a healthcare professional if you are having thoughts of self-harm or suicide. There is no shame in getting help. It takes a courageous, brave person to break through the stigma-laden thoughts around mental health. You are loved, you are wanted, and you have a divine purpose on this planet. If you are having self-harm or suicidal thoughts, please call the US National Suicide Prevention Lifeline at 1-800-273-8255, visit www.suicidepreventionlifeline.org, or reach out to a professional in your local community.

AND THEN CAME SPIRITUALITY

Spiritual awakening is about connecting you with your soul, your spirituality, and it doesn't care what you believe or if you go to church every Sunday. Spirituality does not belong to one religion, spiritual belief, or practice. According to the Oxford dictionary, spirituality is the quality of being concerned with the human spirit or soul as opposed to material or physical things. Spiritual awakening is not about status, material things, or proving your worth. It is about connecting you with your soul and your divine purpose.

WHAT IS SPIRITUAL AWAKENING?

Spiritual awakening is the process of waking up from your life-long conditioning and programming that made you who you have been to this point. It is the beginning of the deconstruction of who you are and how you operate in this world. It is the path to your authentic self, to your power and freedom, to your connection with the Divine, to an intentional and well-lived life, and to enlightenment.

You may have heard whispers over the years that there is more to life than what you were doing. Maybe you were working on a project at work and thought, "This isn't impactful enough. I want to make the world a better place." Perhaps you got a promotion at work only to feel emptiness following the initial excitement. Or maybe you married the partner that made your parents proud and your friends jealous, you bought that dream home, had the family, and you still feel like something big is missing from your life. That is spiritual awakening knocking on your door.

Spiritual awakening makes you question your identity, your purpose, and the meaning of life and death. But it seems that you resisted the urge to make any changes up to this point. Why? Because on paper you have it all? You are incredibly lucky to have a great job, have the people in your life that you do, and you should be grateful for everything you have learned and earned through the blood, sweat, and tears over your life. So, you silenced the whispers.

Then the Divine -- or Universe, God, Goddess, Source, Creator, or Spirit, whichever word you'd like to use for a higher power than you -- got louder. She is loving, kind, and patient. But she doesn't like to be ignored. She tried to get your attention through an unexpected job loss, a new project that went terribly wrong, getting passed up for that promotion, a move that fell through, a breakup or divorce, the loss of a loved one. This was the Divine getting louder. She was trying to tell you that life is short and now is that time wake up so you can fully step into your true self and fulfill your purpose.

Maybe you are stubborn like me and you still resisted. You decided to double down and strive for more. Maybe you went back to school to get an advanced degree (or another one). Maybe you went for that job that seemed out of reach. Maybe you landed your "dream job" and put all of yourself into that. You have a proven track record of your grit, your tenacity, your ability to overcome any challenge that life threw at you. You silenced her again and kept persisting forward in the life you created.

You ignored the Divine's whispers. You missed her signs. You didn't recognize that she was giving you the opportunity to wake up in your time. The Divine took matters into her hands and decided it was time for your crumbling.

The crumbling is when the Divine shocks you into a spiritual awakening. This can include, but is not limited to, the loss of a job that was your identity, the death of the person closest to you, a brush with death yourself, a major accident that changes your way of life, finding out the love of your life is cheating on you, or another event that shocks and rocks your world into an unrecognizable state.

STAGES OF SPIRITUAL AWAKENING

Many people often think that a spiritual awakening is a spontaneous and smooth transition. You may have heard of people like Eckhart Tolle or Byron Katie being at extreme lows in their lives and suddenly awaken to the illusion of their suffering. Then you see how incredible and amazing their lives are now. But most people don't see the roller coaster of a journey that took place to get Tolle and Katie where they are today, nor do most people have a spontaneous awakening. Other people pay attention to the signs from the Divine and wake up on their time without the need for the crumbling. While others, like myself, needed to go through the crumbling to finally wake up. Regardless, of the how, I've identified six stages that people go through during their awakening process.

1. Asleep – Those in the first stage are wrapped up in survival and having their day-to-day needs met. They are surrounded by drama. They feel that life happens to them, often blame others and the world for their problems, and play the victim. They see things as black and white

and follow the rules of society so they can fit in.

2. Striving – People at the second stage realize they have some control over their lives. They are starting to take responsibility for their actions but still get caught in the blame game and conditioned behaviors. They often are striving for more, trying to prove their worth, and are concerned with their status in society.

3. Questioning – People in this stage start to question who they are, what their purpose is, and the meaning of life and death. This is often where the spiritual awakening initiation or crumbling takes place. It is when people start to see through the illusions of our conditioning, programming, and societal influences. They want to take full responsibility for themselves.

4. Seeking – This stage is where people begin searching for truth, purpose, and meaning. They are untangling their belief systems and behaviors to connect with their true selves. They see through the illusion of control, society, and groupthink or mass consciousness. People at this stage often find it hard to integrate their new beliefs

with the world around them and tend to feel lonely.

5. Awake – People in this stage are expressing their true selves and have taken full responsibility for their life, thoughts, and actions. They don't need to prove their worth because they know they and all those around them are worthy. Situations are no longer good or bad, right or wrong. They find peace in accepting what is. The ability and willingness to trust and surrender to the Divine is strengthening.

6. Integration – This is where full enlightenment is reached. People at this stage are in a constant state of flow with life while still participating in the world. They easily allow and accept life to happen for them without binary beliefs or reactions. They fully trust the Divine and their path. Few people reach this stage, and those who have don't shout it from the rooftops.

These stages are not absolute, nor are they like the levels in a video game that once you "pass" a level, you don't ever return to it. They are fluid, and you may experience different stages throughout the day, week, month, or year. However, you will find that you spend more time in the later stages than the earlier stages as you progress in your growth and transformation after a spiritual awakening.

SPIRITUAL AWAKENING SYMPTOMS

Each person's spiritual awakening experience is different and unique to their path. Some people listen to the whispers from the Divine in the first three stages and go through a gradual initiation while others have to go through the crumbling. However you are going through it is perfect for you and your journey.

You might be wondering if what you are experiencing is a spiritual awakening, a mid-life crisis, depression, or the slow descent into insanity. There can be a deep sense of meaninglessness to life when one goes through a crumbling. Spiritual awakening can feel like any and all of these things at once. The Divine needs you cracked open so you can heal and become who you were always meant to be.

The eleven most common symptoms of a spiritual awakening are:

1. Your life feels fake and empty
2. You question your beliefs and behaviors
3. You feel confused, lost, and alone
4. You want more meaning and purpose
5. You crave more solitude

6. You want to live more simply and get rid of "stuff"
7. You start to see through the illusions of society
8. You connect with your feelings and the feelings of others on a much deeper level
9. You have more compassion for all beings and situations
10. You notice synchronicities and recognize patterns all around you
11. You feel connected to everyone and everything

DEATH OF THE EGO

You may have heard of the term known as a Dark Night of the Soul. The term goes with spiritual awakening like peanut butter goes with jelly in most circles. You will assuredly come across it as you are learning about spiritual awakening, so I'll touch on it briefly even though I don't use the term.

The term was originally used in a poem written by the sixteenth-century Spanish mystic and poet St. John of the Cross, though many religions, spiritual practices, teachers, and psychologists use it today. Some would liken it to what I call the crumbling, others call it a spiritual depression. Some believe that everyone goes through the Dark Night of the Soul and others think only some do. But most agree that it is the death of the "ego," or the complete dissolution of the conditioned and programmed beliefs, behaviors, and habits with which you self-identify. I don't use the term Dark Night of the Soul because I believe that everyone who goes through the spiritual awakening goes through the death of the "ego."

WHY SPIRITUAL AWAKENINGS ARE SO HUSH-HUSH

You are feeling alone on this journey right now. You are connecting to feelings and depths that you haven't before. You are defining new levels of vulnerability, and it is terrifying. I get it. I've been there. Many of us are taught that vulnerability is weakness, weakness is a burden, and no one wants to be a burden. We're taught that vulnerability is shameful. Women especially feel this with so many female terms associated with weakness and shame – common phrases (in the U.S.) like "You throw like a girl. You hit like a girl. Pull up your big girl panties. Stop crying. What are you, a girl?" The LGBTQ+ community feels this when the heteronormative insults start flying in response to affection and emotions, mostly among straight men, such as, "Hugging and showing emotions is gay. What a fag. You like his shirt? That's so gay if you tell another dude you love him." All of these are examples that

I've heard with my ears from adults regarding emotions and vulnerability. No wonder people aren't sharing their stories of spiritual awakenings to others who are still stuck in the beliefs that vulnerability is "bad."

Maybe you pushed past the fear and tried talking to friends or loved ones about what was going on with you. But either they don't understand what you are going through, can't relate or empathize with your experience, or brush it off like "everyone feels this way sometimes." People have a hard time understanding why anyone who "has it all" would want to find more meaning and have a bigger impact on the world. So, you start to shut down. Stop talking about it. Maybe even start to believe there is something wrong with you, and now you are stuck in the in-between. Not who you were, but not yet who you are meant to be. But I assure you that you are not alone.

There are millions of people who have gone through this. Many have had similar experiences as you. They felt fear, guilt, and shame about being perceived as weak or crazy. They tried talking to loved ones and got shut down, told they were being silly, crazy, ungrateful, or selfish for wanting something different Lnd more. Those people did one of two things; they found new people to support them on their new journey, or they remained stuck in the in-between because they couldn't move forward, but they certainly couldn't go back to the way life was.

Those who are stuck in the in-between are still living unfulfilling, empty lives. They are feeling more alone, more misunderstood, and more like an outcast with each moment that they stay in limbo. They aren't living their purpose nor are they living a fulfilling life. These people often shut down emotionally. They have a hard time keeping a job or a relationship. They have a hard time making and keeping friends because they don't know who they are or what they can contribute to a relationship. They may be numbing themselves with excessive work, extreme exercise, alcohol, drugs, sex, or other self-medicating behaviors.

But there is another way. Finding your new normal after a spiritual awakening is possible. You can live a life filled with meaning, purpose, fulfillment, joy, love, and freedom. You can break free from the shackles of your conditioning and programming, and you can connect with who you were always meant to be. You can find meaningful work and relationships and surround yourself with the people, places, and things that nourish your soul and give you energy. Since you are here, you have already chosen which path you want to take.

METAMORPHOSIS OF THE BUTTERFLY

Spiritual awakening is often likened to the metamorphosis of the butterfly. I'll demonstrate with the story of the butterfly. You may remember it from science class years ago, but listen to it through the lens of spiritual growth and transformation.

The caterpillar is born from an egg, then eats its egg and the leaf on which it was born to begin to grow big and strong. It goes from one leaf to the next, eating, dodging birds and children that may cause it harm, growing, shedding its exoskeleton, and eating some more. As the caterpillar continues to grow, it just does what it was programmed to do by nature. It doesn't question life or why it is the way it is. It doesn't question why it can't fly like some other insects or animals. It just keeps eating from leaf to leaf, day after day. Until one day, it wakes up and realizes it suddenly has this incredible need to climb a branch and hang upside down.

From the inside out, the caterpillar begins to become the chrysalis. It twists and wriggles, shedding its caterpillar skin for the last time until all that is left is a chrysalis hanging from a branch. Inside the chrysalis, the old form begins to dissolve into a goo, completely unrecognizable from its old form. From limbs or organs, the caterpillar is no more. And then something magical happens. From the dissolved remains of the caterpillar, a beautiful form begins to take shape. The shape of the butterfly. This is where you may think the transformation is over. But it isn't.

Now, the butterfly has fully formed inside of the

chrysalis, but it has yet to emerge. This is one of the most important stages of the metamorphosis. The butterfly goes through great struggle to break out of and free from the chrysalis. Squeezing its large body out of the tiny hole for a long time, with no mouth to help eat its way out. This struggle plays an important role in the development of the butterfly. It helps move essential fluids from the body to the wings. Once the butterfly emerges from the chrysalis, its wings are still small, crumpled, and wet, making it extremely vulnerable to predators since it can't fly yet. Then, the butterfly begins to flap its wings, not for the purpose of flight, but for the purpose of moving blood and fluids into the wings so they become full, strong, and dry. Only after the complete dissolution of its prior form, the great struggle of getting out of the chrysalis, and working hard to strengthen the wings is the butterfly able to take flight.

There is another story of a boy who comes across a butterfly struggling to get out of the chrysalis. The story has been told many ways and I'm not sure where it originated. A variation of it, perhaps even the original, was in Frank Dupree's book *Metamorphosis*. I'll share a variation of the story below.

There was a boy that came across a butterfly struggling to get out of a chrysalis. The boy watched as the butterfly, no longer with its caterpillar mouth, tried as it might to get out of the constraints of the shell of its former self. The boy began to feel sad and wanted to help. The boy pulled out his pocketknife and carefully cut open the chrysalis without cutting the butterfly. He excitedly watched as the butterfly crawled out of the shell with much more ease. But he saw that something was off. The butterfly's body was swollen, and its wings were small and crumpled. Despite the butterfly's best efforts, its wings wouldn't grow. It could barely drag its body along, and soon the butterfly died. The boy was eager to ease the struggle and suffering of the butterfly. But he didn't realize that the butterfly needed to struggle through the small opening in the chrysalis to move the fluid and blood from the body to the wings.

Both of these stories illustrate the destruction, struggle, and transformation of spiritual awakening. This is your metamorphosis. You walked through life before your spiritual awakening not thinking much about why you did what you did or believed in what you believed in. Until one day, there is something inside of you that changes. That thing calls you to do something different, to think differently, to believe differently, but you aren't sure what yet. You enter the time of transformation – you become the chrysalis. In the chrysalis, who you were will completely dissolve into an unrecognizable form – you will un-become everything that you were taught to be. You will go through great struggles, confusion, and times of pain that you will want to bypass or have someone save you from. But it is through your greatest struggles that you will heal and become the beautiful, unique, strong creature that can take flight and create the life you never imagined possible. I know because I've been there and have been grateful to be there for others going through it too.

2

MY RUDE AWAKENING

"We can never obtain peace in the outer world until we make peace with ourselves."

— HIS HOLINESS, THE DALAI LAMA XIV

SPIRITUAL BEGINNINGS

Growing up, I was the kid running around barefoot in the woods. I was highly creative with a wildly active imagination. I was always full of energy despite my family's best efforts to tame me. By first grade, I was convinced I was a witch and told my two best friends, Becky and Travis, that the wind whispered to me when I closed my eyes and emptied my head. They of course made fun of me by blowing in my hair when I tried to demonstrate what I meant on the playground.

Shortly thereafter, I was writing in my Charlie Brown journal about how I wasn't from this planet, and I was placed here with "this family" to try to help them. But I didn't want this assignment anymore and I wanted to go home. By age nine, I started to be "chased" by spirits. I know now they were simply trying to communicate with me. But back then, electronics and water would do strange things when I was around. Turning on and off. Flickering. Things that terrified me for many years until I realized what was happening. By sixth grade, I was going to the library (internet didn't exist then) and checking out books about "fringe" spiritual practices and beliefs. Energy healing. Psychic abilities. Tarot. Astrology. Palmistry. I even did a school report on Voodoo in middle school. Going into high school, my friends would describe me as "spiritual." I would hang out at the local Barnes & Noble in the "New Age" and "Spirituality" sections reading and learning as much as I could about other beliefs and practices. At sixteen, I met my soulmate friend who was probably the first person to understand me. We meditated, created altars in our rooms, shared what we learned and experienced. But then life happened.

My parents were getting divorced and I was moving in with my sister and her fiancé. The summer before my senior year of high school, I started paying rent, bills, and buying groceries. I had to "be responsible." I still participated in the usual teenage shenanigans, but by seventeen, I started taking psychedelic mushrooms to connect with Spirit while my friends were using them for recreation. The pressures of life just got heavier after I graduated. My on-again-off-again boyfriend was a local drug dealer who was addicted to meth and not wanting me to move on. My parents were dealing with their divorce, my sister and her then-husband were dealing with their mess of a relationship (now divorced), I was in year three of my eating disorder. Things felt like they couldn't get much worse. And a lifeline came. One of my sister's friends reached out to me to offer me her couch. With 200 bucks, my clothes, and the car I bought the year prior, I headed to the big city to escape the insanity and find my way.

My spiritual awakening story is what led me to write this book. I don't want anyone else to feel as lost, scared, ungrateful, shameful, or on a lonely island like I did. I felt like I didn't have anyone in my life that understood what I was going through. Friends were as supportive as they could be, but said things like, "Maybe you need a new job," "Take a vacation," "That sounds rough" or one that said she was feeling the same but then just went to another company and found herself in the same situation. My partner said, "Everyone goes through that sometimes." And most of my family couldn't relate because they thought I "had it all."

THE WHISPERS

As life continued, my spiritual pursuits took a backseat. I started to follow the path of the masses. I worked, I went to school, I dated, I had friends. I did all the things I "should" do. Maybe not in the traditional sense, but I did them my way. I worked hard, and I played hard. I heard the Divine whisper to me, but I tried brushing Her off.

First was leaving my first "adult" job without another job lined up when the market tanked in 2008. I knew that anything was better than the work environment in which I was at the time. I felt in my bones there was more for me than this. While I was strong enough to take the leap, I was still stifled by fear to explore another direction than the one I was on. I've heard my whole life that your value and worthiness is tied to how much money you make. My partner at the time provided evidence to this belief by threatening to leave me. I needed to find another job that gave me the opportunity to grow my skillset and my bank account so I could be worthy of love and acceptance. So, I did.

In spring of that year, my partner-at-the-time and I bought a house. As we were walking through the home, I got a feeling that someone died there. So, I asked the realtor. My partner told the realtor, "Don't mind her. She's crazy." We bought the house and moved in, and I started seeing and hearing things in my imagination. I told my partner, and he of course brushed it off. Then the new neighbor asked if I was experiencing anything weird. She went on to tell me that the previous owner, before the house was flipped, died in the kitchen. Suddenly everything I was seeing, feeling, and hearing made sense and was validated. My gifts started to become stronger and "stranger" things were happening on a regular basis. Someone even called me a medium. But I didn't "see" dead people as they showed in the movies, so I "knew" I wasn't a medium. I again decided to ignore what was going on and continued my socially acceptable and parental approved life.

Next came my eating disorder treatment. I struggled with bulimia and anorexia since I was fourteen. When I turned twenty-three, I put on sixty pounds in six months. Fast forward to 2007, my (now ex) partner said he wanted out of the relationship if I didn't lose weight. The Divine was telling me that I wasn't on the right path or with the right person. I thought the solution was to go to treatment because I had "burned out my metabolism," and I had committed to this person, so I needed to try everything I could to save the marriage. Over those six months, I had the opportunity to process and heal from childhood trauma, sexual assault, self-loathing, and more. The Divine was saying that it was time for me to deconstruct who I thought I was so I could find out who I was meant to me. But I wasn't ready yet. Even after the divorce, a lot of healing took place. A lot was deconstructed. But I wasn't ready to go deep enough to break through to the other side.

The Divine tried getting my attention again when my (new) partner and I found out we couldn't have kids. We went through fertility testing. I tried holistic means to get pregnant. But it wasn't happening for us. We tried adopting and that fell through twice with the same family. I thought to myself, "Maybe we are made for a different path." But I continued on the same path. Working more. Striving harder. Leaning into what I could control and what I thought would bring me happiness and fulfillment. I dabbled in intuitive development books and I went through Reiki 1 training. But then I put those things aside to focus on my responsibilities and started numbing out more. The Divine decided to get louder.

In 2013, my partner and I were laid off at the same time. It was like a big reset. Being financially prudent, we were set up to take our time to figure out what was next. I hired a life coach to help me get clear on what I wanted and create a plan to get there. It included eventually becoming a life coach, but in five or so years. I did a life coaching business plan for my final project for my bachelor's degree, but I felt like I needed more experience and a master's degree before I was ready to make the move. My coach tried pushing me on it, but I wasn't ready. The fear, programming, and conditioning took over again. I applied for grad school and got another corporate job. I thought, "I'm happiest learning new things and helping others develop." I convinced myself again. It is true that I love leading teams, learning new skills, and having new experiences. It was the way in which I was doing it that wasn't aligned with my soul.

No matter how much I tried to convince myself that living the societal dream would fulfill me, it didn't take long before I was miserable again. I remember reviewing a strategy that one of my team members put together and thinking to myself, "Wow. What is this for? None of this matters. We're just pushing pills." But I again persisted. I finished my MBA, got recruited by Amazon, and thought, "This is it. This is what I've been working so hard for." So me, my partner, and our three fur babies packed up and moved west.

MY CRUMBLING

I was a self-proclaimed workaholic and wino for many years. I used it to numb myself from my feelings of frustration, unfulfillment, and a lifetime of pain. My numbing was at its peak around the second year at Amazon. I was working crazy hours and coming home to drink a bottle of wine to numb myself from the stress and emptiness I was feeling. I completely disconnected from my emotions, body, and spirit. I didn't trust anyone else, let alone myself. I thought I'd eventually find happiness if I just kept pushing myself to do and achieve more. But I became numb to even the things I was achieving. No matter how big or small the achievement, it was just another task to check off on my never-ending list of things to accomplish. I would move on to the next thing without celebration and often little to no acknowledgment.

I had recently gone to a new team with an awesome manager and new people to lead and develop. I loved my team. My hours were more reasonable for the first time in my entire career, and I was making great money. I couldn't have asked for a better group of people to work with. I was learning new things, and I was hoping this was going to finally feel like enough. And then the floor broke out from underneath me.

My maternal grandmother unexpectedly died. She was my rock. The woman who supported me through anything and everything. The one who told me not to care or worry about what anyone else thought because I am perfect the way I am. While I knew her health had been deteriorating, I thought I had more time with her. But I didn't. I came out of a meeting and checked my phone, and I had a text message saying that she had died.

About a month later, my partner and I were having adult beverages out on the patio, talking about the probable upcoming funeral of my paternal grandmother. Our Great Dane Lab mix, Roger, jumped off the patio and yelped as he crashed down. We brought him to the vet ER where he was diagnosed with a terminal, aggressive bone cancer. After a week of spoiling him as much as possible, we had to put him down.

A few weeks after that, my paternal grandmother died. We knew that her time was limited, but it didn't make it any easier. She was the woman who taught me about the wisdom in the woods, and the reason I spent so much time in the woods as a child. She nurtured my imagination and infused play into everything we did. Whether we made a fort out of chairs and blankets, played jacks on the floor, or picked flowers with gratitude from the forest behind her house and pressed them in wax paper, life was filled with wonder and joy.

The pain of losing these three over three months was more than I have ever felt. It was indescribable. It broke me open. It created the disruption in my programming and conditioning that allowed the Divine to get through. I started questioning everything. Why was doing what I was doing both personally and professionally? Why did I believe what I believed? Who do these beliefs belong to? What do I believe about life, death, and God? What do I believe about who I am? "Wait – who am I?" Nothing made sense anymore. But I didn't know what to do. I tried to go about my day as usual, but there was no such thing anymore. I started on my spiritual awakening journey and I was all-in.

CHANGING COURSE

The first thing I did was quit drinking. I didn't know I was going through a spiritual awakening yet, but I knew that I wanted to reconnect with my emotions, begin to work through the decades of stuffed, repressed emotions, and start healing. I didn't feel like I knew much, but I did realize I had a lot of work to do. I started with the thirty-day Alcohol Experiment with Annie Grace from ThisNakedMind.com. I got her book *This Naked Mind* and dedicated the next thirty days to deconstructing my beliefs and behaviors with alcohol. Those thirty days just continued, and I've been alcohol-free since June 4, 2017. Then I had the overwhelming desire to get rid of everything.

I normally purge my closet every six months, but this was another level. I wanted to get rid of everything that no longer brought me joy. Suddenly, there were a lot of things that no longer brought me joy. Much of what I had just became stuff, and I didn't want stuff clogging my space. I didn't realize it at the time, but this is a natural part of the awakening process. We're groomed to want and acquire more things because that is tied to success. My definition of value and success changed dramatically. I got rid of furniture, clothes, decorations, houseware, anything that we didn't need to be happy was on the chopping block. It felt so freeing to declutter and donate so much to others that would find joy and happiness in those things.

My love of learning has always been a theme in my life. I'm a naturally curious person, so it wasn't a surprise when I dove headfirst into reading and workshops. I thought maybe I just needed to figure out my purpose. But I quickly realized I couldn't find my purpose if I didn't know who I was. I had to backtrack and start digging into who I became. But who was I if I wasn't this person that took nearly thirty-eight years (at that time) to create? That's when I realized I was going through a spiritual awakening. I started exploring the eight limbs of yoga, Buddhism, shamanism, sound healing. I took the next level Reiki training. I learned other forms of energy healing. I took a watercolor class to reconnect with my creative side, started going to drum circles and participated in Solstice, Earth Magic, and Shamanic ceremonies. I was exploring different beliefs and practices that resonated with my soul.

I started writing for myself because I wanted to document what I was going through. Funny enough, I thought it might be useful down the road to reflect on my experience. I explored my thoughts, feelings, and experiences throughout the day to understand why I was feeling and reacting the way I was. I started reaching out to those around me to find community with others that have been through or were going through something similar. I reached out to friends, family, and coworkers who seemed fairly progressive and open-minded. Most people didn't know how to respond. They'd give me resources for exploring careers, suggest a good therapist, or brush it off as "everyone feels this way from time to time." Those people closest to me shared a similar sentiment, "I don't understand what you are going through but let me know how I can help you." My dear friend Jen sent me a beautiful gratitude journal which was probably the thing that helped me get through the tough days the most. Many have said, and I can attest to, you can't be in a state of suffering when you are in a state of gratitude. I love this quote from an anonymous source, "Gratitude turns what we have into enough." I was learning what that meant on a soul level.

My thoughts, feelings, reactions, and actions toward others changed. The family drama that used to bother me became white noise. I no longer got angry or frustrated in a reactive, explosive way. I adopted the belief that when someone is triggered, it is about them and not about me. When I get triggered, it is about me, not the other person. As I practiced this belief, I started to see through their anger or tantrum to see a person that was in pain and was scared. I also set boundaries for those who wanted to complain about their situations or played the victim but continued to put themselves in those situations and with those people who they claimed to be harming them. I realized I didn't need to keep giving my energy to those who weren't willing to give a fair exchange of energy. So I stopped.

I can't say that one book, class, workshop, podcast, movie, or other "thing" helped me. My conditioning and programming were deep, and I'm pretty stubborn. But somewhere along the way, I decided to pick up my spiritual practice again. And just that decision was the first step toward my true self that I needed to take. It lit me up again. While I felt uncomfortable telling people what I was up to, the spiritual exploration energized me and gave me things to look forward to. I was consuming books by spiritual teachers like water. I was attending workshops every weekend I could. I started traveling with the purpose of spiritual growth and education. I worked with a variety of healers, spiritual practitioners and coaches. I met and continue to meet my soul family through these experiences.

In the two years following my spiritual awakening crumbling, I built my tool kit to help myself and others through this process. I finished my Reiki Master training, completed two years of Shamanic Practitioner training, learned about Human Design, reconnected with and, more importantly, embraced my intuitive gifts. I earned two life coaching certifications, one of which is tailored for people going through spiritual awakening and those choosing to walk a spiritual life. I had a brush with mortality as I faced possible breast cancer. I had emergency gallbladder surgery in the middle of writing my first book, *The Art of Connected Leadership*. I left my corporate job to start my leadership coaching practice.

Let me repeat that.

I spent two years dedicated to spirituality and my spiritual growth and transformation, but my first coaching practice was to help corporate managers. Talk about resistance. I was still holding on to the person I had been because my old programming and conditioning didn't let me see a way that spirituality could be more than my nights, weekends, and vacations.

COURSE CORRECTION

Luckily, I met and hired this "business coach" to help me work through my blocks. She was a little "woo-woo" which is why I hired her. She read chakras, the seven main energy centers in the body. She asked me why I am focused on leadership coaching when I spend all my time learning about, practicing, and sharing gems about spirituality. Mind blown. "You mean, I can do that?" To which she replied, "Why did you hire me?" Point proven.

Part of my course correction was reconnecting

with my intuitive gifts and creativity. I started offering what I call Soul readings which are a combination of Oracle cards, energy reading, and mediumship; offering energy healing; coaching people on their spiritual journeys; and blogging on spirituality. I continue to develop my intuitive gifts, and I am dedicated to my continued growth and transformation. I worked with an incredible intuitive mentor who helped me realize I can connect with souls that have died. Reading about my youth, you may think, "Well, of course." But I didn't know what it was until I had the right people to help me understand what my gifts were. Yes, I finally admitted I'm a medium. Who knew? Okay, besides all of the people who told me that over the years.

It hasn't been easy, and there have been many times I resisted letting go of who I was. I still face fear and resistance every day. Every time fear starts to get the best of me, or someone I love asks me why I can't just go back to the way things were or asks if this is temporary, the Divine reminds me that there is no going back. I work through the resistance -- mine and the resistance of others wanting me to stay the same. The "business" coach that I invested in to help me move past my resistance empowered me to give myself permission to be me in all my glory and not worry about what is next. I've learned that we don't always know where the path will lead but it becomes clearer with each step we take. Even though

I continue to change and evolve personally and professionally, the one constant is my desire to help people grow and transform.

Today, I help people navigate their spiritual awakening, integrate their new beliefs and behaviors into their lives, and continue to empower them on their personal and spiritual growth journeys. I do this through transformational coaching that incorporates Human Design, energy healing, and intuitive and Oracle card readings. I integrate these modalities as I've found that different tools are needed at different times as people are reconnecting with their true selves, letting go of and healing their pasts. I love helping people discover what makes them happy and fulfilled, what gives them purpose, and helps them to achieve their definition of a life well-lived. I hope to do the same for you in the following chapters by giving you the information and tools that can help you adjust to life after your spiritual awakening.

3

THE JOURNEY AHEAD

"Sometimes the longest journey we make is the sixteen inches from our heads to our hearts."

— ELENA AVILA

A spiritual awakening can be the loneliest and most challenging journey of your life, but it doesn't have to be. Together, I can help you move forward with your new beliefs and create a fulfilling life of joy, love, and freedom. You will learn how to create lasting changes so you don't fall back into old habits. You'll be able to surround yourself with the love and support you crave, and you'll be able to navigate your spiritual growth ahead with confidence. This is not an easy road. It takes time, practice, patience, and compassion for yourself and others. Going back to the way life was isn't an option. I'll be with you in the following chapters, cheering you on, reminding you that you're not alone and that you can find a magical life after your spiritual awakening.

WHERE YOU'RE GOING

The spiritual awakening process is hard. I know I keep saying this, but it is important that you know it isn't going to be a quick fix. There is little instant gratification on this journey. But the reward is worth the work. It is okay to revert to old behaviors once in awhile. It means that there is more for you to learn and heal from in this area. Just keep going.

This book is a transformational experience. It is based on my experience, education, training, teaching, coaching, and healing experiences. There will be things that resonate and inspire you and things that won't. That is perfectly okay. A spiritual awakening is not a one-size-fits-all experience. Take what works for you and feel free to tweak or toss the concepts that don't.

Over the next several chapters, you're going to explore and participate in the tools and practices that I've personally and professionally used, along with stories from people who I've helped to adjust to life after a spiritual awakening. I encourage you to read these chapters in order because the concepts, tools, and practices build on each other. However, you know what is best for yourself. If you are going through a lot of personal resistance now, skip to chapter 7 to help you work through the resistance. This book can be used as a reference guide along your journey. There will be writing and reflection exercises along the way. I encourage you to get a journal dedicated to this work. I also encourage putting pen to paper instead of typing. There is something magical that happens in the brain when you write things out.

The journey ahead is an exciting one. You uncover your personal power, what lights you up, and helps you eliminate the things that don't. It will give you the opportunity to create the life that you want without the constraints of someone or something else.

In Chapter 4, you'll learn about the programming and conditioning that we all go through as part of our human experience. You'll start to understand why you believe what you believe and decide if you still believe it. This chapter has your first writing and reflection exercise to start diving deep into yourself.

Chapter 5 is all about healing from past wounds so that you can create the space for new beliefs and behaviors. You'll explore your shadow, understand the illusion of control, get your first of many tools to help you understand how the stories you tell yourself impact your reality, and learn about the freedom of forgiveness. You'll also work through three shadow work tools to help you with self-talk, self-sabotaging, and triggers, and we'll end with a simple but powerful releasing ritual.

Chapter 6 will help you decide what you want less or more of as you reconnect with your true self and bring yourself closer to a life well-lived. You'll understand the role of expectations; yours and others. You'll learn about the potential changes that may take place as you step more fully into your true self and the power of letting go. You'll also do an exercise that will help you reconnect with the things that truly bring you fulfillment and joy.

Chapter 7 will help you work through resistance to change from those around you and yourself. I'll review the basics to help you navigate the inevitable resistance and share with you examples of the types of resistance you'll face from others and yourself. You'll be reminded of the importance of self-care, and I'll share some helpful breathwork exercises when you get stressed, anxious, or are feeling over-whelmed. You'll finish this chapter with some reflection journaling about your resistance and self-care exercise.

Chapter 8 is all about intuition and using it as a guide to help you in your new life. I'll discuss masculine and feminine energies and what happens when they are out of balance. You'll learn about empathic abilities, the five clairs, intuitive development tools, and manifestation, and I'll walk you through a meditation to ground and clear your energy. This chapter ends with a reflection and journaling exercise.

Chapter 9 focuses on helping you find your soul family and the support you will want on this journey. You'll learn about the different types and forms of teachers you may want to work with and how to find the right one for you. I'll share some resources for finding the types of friends you want in your circle. You'll end the chapter with a values exercise to prioritize the values in your life and relationships after your spiritual awakening.

Chapter 10 gives you some insights into what you can expect as you continue on your spiritual growth path. You'll learn about the power of being in the present moment, understand the guideposts to know if you are living in alignment with your life or not. You'll also understand the power of gratitude and, potentially most importantly, fun.

Throughout the book, I'll share stories from clients and my spiritual awakening experience. These stories are meant to help illustrate the types of experiences you might also go through on your journey to adjust to life after a spiritual awakening. Everyone's experience is unique to their journeys and lessons, so don't worry about doing it "right" or "wrong" if something doesn't make sense for you. You are exactly where you need to be and are going through exactly what you need to be going through for your growth.

ROADBLOCKS

We all know how hard it is to create and sustain new habits. Spiritual awakening is like creating new habits on steroids. Not only will you feel moments of confusion along the way, but people around you will too. People don't like change even if the change is for the highest and greatest good. You are going to meet resistance from some of the people around you. People who want you to stay exactly how they know you to be. You are also going to face your resistance. Resistance that feels so real but is just your ego's way of trying to keep you safe. You're going to face doubt and fear. You may lose friends, family connections, or romantic relationships. This is normal, though I know firsthand how painful it can be. There are going to be times where you will question if you can go back to the way things were. Wonder if all of this is worth it. It is going to get extremely uncomfortable. You have to get uncomfortable to grow. The good news is that you already are uncomfortable. Find comfort in the discomfort because being uncomfortable with the unknown is better than being miserable with the known. You'll learn to have gratitude for the discomfort because that feeling is how you know you are growing and transforming.

THIS IS AWAKENING

Tina was a brilliant, lovely young woman who initially came to me to figure out her career path. She was fired from a job that she made her identity. She was ashamed that she lost her job for a silly mistake that she didn't know why she even made. Her parents were so proud of her for getting that job, and now they were trying to involve themselves in her finances and plan, and they were pressuring her to figure it out quickly since losing the job. She was stuck on how she let her parents down and she didn't know who she was without the status of her former role.

Through our work together, we discovered that she was tying her career status to the love and worthiness of her parents and uncovered an unconscious belief that if she wasn't successful enough, her parents would leave her. She was adopted, something that she did not think much of previously nor even talk about until we were a few sessions into working together. But as we worked to unravel this belief, we spent time healing her wounds that she didn't know she was harboring from being adopted as an infant. She identified her stories, feelings, and beliefs that supported the concept that her parents wouldn't want her if she wasn't successful.

I taught her different techniques and tools to help her change the stories and build more productive

behavioral patterns. We used neuroplasticity techniques (science!) to change how she acted and
responded to things her parents said and did. She
also implemented healthy boundaries with her
parents to give her the space and freedom to be
herself and maintain a good relationship with them.
This didn't happen overnight.

It took awareness, with willingness to dig deep to
understand what was going on. It took practice and
compassion for herself and her parents so she could
break free from her conditioning to create a life that
was aligned with who she was. While she came to
me about her career, she quickly realized she was
going through an awakening process.

Our work together changed from what was next
for her career to helping her through the awakening
process and finding her true self. She was committed
to this work because she knew she couldn't go back
to the way things were. She was ready to let go of
the pressure and expectations that she put on herself
to fit this idea of who she was supposed to be and
become the person she was always meant to be.

4

THE UN-BECOMING

"Maybe the journey isn't so much about becoming anything. Maybe it's about un-becoming everything that isn't you, so you can be who you were meant to be in the first place."

— PAULO COELHO

You are already in a state of un-becoming. You see the cracks in your beliefs, and you are questioning everything. That's okay because most of your beliefs aren't yours anyway. In this chapter, you are going to explore where programming and conditioning comes from, why you believe the things you do, and we'll dive deep to understand what you truly believe with your first writing exercise.

WHO BELIEVES THIS STUFF ANYWAY?

Your thoughts, beliefs, and behaviors primarily come from the programming and conditioning you receive in the first seven to eight years of your life. They belong to your parents, siblings, family, friends, teachers, mentors, society, and others. And most of their beliefs aren't theirs either. Think about that for a moment. What you were taught about life and death, love and war, right and wrong, what it means to be successful or not all came from someone else who learned it from someone else who learned it from someone else and so on. Most of what you believe are recycled beliefs from several generations back.

You and everyone else are conditioned and programmed to believe and behave the way you have been operating. You were taught what is acceptable in your home, your schools, at work, and in society. The systems you grew up in have created your ways of thinking and believing without realizing that these are not your own. How you feel about money, what you should study in school, where you should live, having kids, your gender role, who you should or shouldn't date or marry and a million other thoughts and beliefs that shape who you are and what you stand for in the world aren't your own. Talk about disempowering. Let's understand this better so you can take your power back.

I wrote a blog post in 2019, "You are what you consume – seven steps towards consumption awareness," about how you are the combination of what you see, hear, say, feel, touch or what touches you, and the people with whom you surround yourself. You are consciously and unconsciously consuming information all the time, and our minds, bodies, and nervous systems are being impacted. The things you "consume" are impacting us on an energetic level but most of us still haven't realized it yet.

My own programming and conditioning have had lingering effects on me even with the dedicated effort to unravel it all. From childhood, I was naturally a silly, happy child who was bubbling over with energy. But growing up in the midwest with parents who were raised with traditional gender roles from the fifties, I was always told to calm down. Be quiet. Go run around the block so I could come back and "behave." Kids could be around if they were quiet, still, and did exactly as the adults told us. I was also naturally independent. I ran around the woods by myself. I preferred to do chores by myself, and I wasn't a great sharer. In preschool, my classmate asked if she could help me clean off the table. I said, "No, thank you." And continued about my task. The teacher told me it was important that I learn to share, include others, and let people help me.

My parents' beliefs, wounds, and behaviors unintentionally instilled beliefs of not being enough and even being innately wrong within me. Growing up, my mom always compared us to other families. What we had, what we didn't have, the way we looked, how "accomplished" we were. I learned that to get love, I needed to be better than the people she compared us to. This wasn't ever her intention. This is what she learned from her parents and she found evidence to support this belief. As a child, my brain processed what I saw and heard, connected those dots, created the belief, and then found evidence to support and confirm the belief that I needed to do more, achieve more, and make more money to be worthy of love. My dad had strong, negative beliefs about women. Woman couldn't control themselves, they lied, cheated, and manipulated to get what they wanted when they wanted no matter who was hurt along the way. He learned this from his dad and found lots of evidence to support his beliefs. As a child, I translated this to loathing the fact that I was a girl, and so I had to be in extra control of myself. Again, this was not my dad's intended outcome, but it is how it manifested in me. Like my parents, I found the evidence to support my beliefs about what made me worthy of love and that being a girl and a women was a bad thing. Our brains are designed to seek and find the evidence that confirms, supports, and reinforces our beliefs. No matter if that belief is misguided or not.

My family also made it unintentionally clear that

we were to date within our race and it was not acceptable for any of us kids to be gay or bisexual (as if it was a choice). It was okay for others to date who they wanted, but not for me or my siblings. This was decades ago and some of their beliefs have changed since then. But these impressions still have lingering effects on me today.

The people you surround yourself with have an enormous impact on your behaviors, thoughts, what you say, and how you treat other people. According to motivational speaker Jim Rohn, "You are the average of the five people you spend the most time with." A Harvard study done by Dr. David McClelland found that ninety-five percent of your success or failure in life is determined by the people you habitually associate with. They create your conditioned beliefs, behaviors, and habits that you self-identify with. They create your ego. Think about that for a minute. Who do you spend the most time with? Are they people you want to have that much influence on your life? Or do you need to reevaluate who you are spending your time with, personally and professionally?

As I discussed in Chapter 1, your ego is the conditioned and programmed beliefs, behaviors, and habits with which you self-identify. It is here to keep you safe, but it comes from a place of fear and lack. Back in the days of cavemen, the ego kept you safe from the saber tooth tiger through fight, flight, or freeze. When you survived the day, your ego created a neural pathway, or connection, in the brain to unconsciously encourage you to do the same thing you did yesterday so you stay alive. Only today, the saber tooth tiger is your commute to work, your boss, the presentation, the workout, your partner, your kids, or your in-laws. The more that you repeat the things that kept you alive, the deeper the neural pathway becomes in your brain. This is why breaking habits or trying to create new ones is so hard. It takes recognizing the pattern or habit, deciding how you want to change it, and then lots and lots of practice changing our thoughts, feelings, actions, and reactions to the trigger that caused the behavior in the first place. That's where people get tripped up. Humans like instant gratification, especially in today's two-hour delivery world. Luckily, you have your higher self to help remind you along the way what you want if only you listen to it.

Your Higher Self is your true self. Many spiritual beliefs refer to the Higher Self, and it has been called other names such as the inner Self, Soul, Christ-consciousness, Beloved, Buddha-nature, and Spirit. The Higher Self is the part of you that is divine, whole, wise, connected to the collective conscious, and unconditionally loving. It is free from conditioned fears, limiting beliefs, wounds, and ego. Everyone has access to their Higher Selves, including you; however, most people, and most likely you, have blocked, detached from, or denied this side of yourself and you allowed your ego to run the show. Disconnecting from your Higher Self can lead to living your life as others want you to and becoming a people pleaser. This increases stress, anxiety, depression, dis-ease, and more. Reconnecting to your Higher Self can bring the opposite of the disconnected symptoms. I'll talk more about reconnecting with our higher selves in subsequent chapters. Right now, let's start by getting clear on what you believe and why.

PRACTICE MAKES PERFECT

James came to me because he went through a major breakup that left him spinning. This wasn't a normal breakup that leaves someone heartbroken for a few months. This breakup made him question who he was, what his purpose was, and who he wanted to be in the world. In other words, this breakup initiated his spiritual awakening.

James and I started to unpack how he showed up in relationships – romantic and platonic. He realized that he would become whomever the person across the table wanted him to be. Whether it was a friend, a parent, or a partner, he molded to what they wanted him to be so they would love him. He learned early on in life that people "loved" him more when he behaved in a way that made the other person happy. This is a common conditioning that many people have. That's why we have so many people-pleasers in the world. He was also told that he was too sensitive, too emotional, and that he lost relationships, including the now ex-girlfriend with whom he thought was building a future. He learned to stuff his emotions so as not to make others uncomfortable. However, he would explode once his emotions couldn't be stuffed anymore.

Once we figured out why he was shapeshifting for others and hiding his emotions, we spent a lot of time coaching and doing inner child healing around it. After working with me and a therapist for several months, James was able to see his empathic abilities as a gift. They were his superpowers that enabled him to connect with people on a level that most can't. As time went on, James started dating someone new, but it didn't last because he hadn't broken out of the conditioned behaviors yet. He realized that he started to mold into what the other person liked and wanted instead of being his authentic self. The next time it happened, he was able to catch himself doing it during the relationship. Now, he catches himself when he has the thought or feeling to compromise himself for someone else.

Through this coaching and healing work, James was able to gain clarity on how he wanted to contribute to the world and use his incredible empathic abilities. He completed his coach training certification and now helps others heal from challenging breakups and move forward with confidence. He was able to use his experience, lessons, and healing from his spiritual awakening initiated by his breakup to help others. It took identification, healing, awareness, practice, patience, and, most importantly, compassion for himself as he deprogrammed his beliefs and habits to create the life aligned with his true self.

LET YOUR CURIOSITY RUN WILD

This is the first of many writing exercises. Get your journal and writing utensil. I want to set a few ground rules before you start answering the prompts. Rule number one – don't censor yourself. If you want to get the most out of this journey, it is imperative that you feel into the deepest depths to get to the root of the situation. It is your choice whether you want to share this with anyone. I recommend not sharing so you don't feel the extra pressure to say the "right" thing the "right" way or worrying about hurting someone's feelings. This is your journal. Rule number two – be honest. Lying is only going to hurt you. Again, this isn't about saying the "right" thing. No one is going to prove this, give you feedback, or judge you. That brings me to rule number three – no judgment. Release yourself from the judgments about the who, what, where, and why.

You are on this journey to understand, not to blame and not to play the victim. This is about taking responsibility for yourself and your life. Now that I have that covered -- no censoring, be honest, and no judging -- let's begin. Below are the first set of questions I want you to write about and reflect on.

1. What did your parents or guardians teach you about having and expressing emotions?
2. How do you express your feelings? Where did you learn to express your feelings that way?
3. What feelings are you not comfortable expressing? Why?
4. What are your beliefs about money? Where did those beliefs come from?
5. What are some of your beliefs about other races? Where did those beliefs come from?
6. What are some of your beliefs about your identified gender? Where did those beliefs come from?

If you feel called to, question and write about other core beliefs that you have about yourself, others, or life. Success, religions, relationships, and work are great starting areas as well. Ask yourself where your belief came from to help you understand why you believe that way. Get bonus points by using the iterative and interrogative cause and effect technique called "five whys," often used in business to understand the root cause of something by asking "why" five times. Who did it come from and why? Where did they get it from and why? Again, leave judgments at the door. You just want to build awareness right now.

CHECKING IN

This first chapter can be a lot for someone who has just started their internal transformation. If that's you, know that everything you are feeling right now is okay. You just started to explore the depths of your un-becoming. You explored where your programming and conditioning came from. You just dug into why you believed the things you did and gained clarity about what you truly believe in your first writing exercise. Take a breath, take a break, and give yourself some extra care and attention tonight as you process what you've discovered.

5

HEALING IS A FOUR-LETTER WORD

*"Only when we are brave enough to explore the darkness
will we discover the infinite power of our light."*

— BRENÉ BROWN

You may have uncovered a lot of thoughts and beliefs that weren't your own through the writing exercise in the last chapter. You may have also discovered some "dark" thoughts, emotions, behaviors, patterns, and situations that are rooted in the programming and conditioning from your youth – called your shadow. This can be alarming and make you feel disempowered. As with any behavior, pattern, or situation, you take your power back and break the subconscious programming once you become aware (conscious) of it. Then you have three choices if you don't like it: change it, change your thought about it, or choose to accept it and choose to continue your suffering. But the choice is yours. Part of your work as a spiritual being, and especially important during your spiritual awakening, is to look at and integrate your shadow.

You are about to do some self-healing work so you can create the space for new beliefs and behaviors. You are going to explore your shadow, understand the illusion of control, use the first of many tools to help you understand how the stories you tell yourself are reflected in your reality, and learn about the freedom of forgiveness. At the end of this chapter, you'll get an opportunity to work through three shadow work tools to help you with self-talk, self-sabotaging, and triggers, and you will end this chapter with a simple but powerful releasing ritual.

SHADOW WORK

Your shadow is the "dark side" of yourself that causes you to feel shame, fear, unworthiness, and makes you feel like a terrible human being. Your shadow is the deep part of yourself that is often subconscious (or unknown) and is counter to the image you want to project to the world. Most of your shadow was programmed and conditioned in you at a young age by your family and caretakers.

Many people deny, suppress, or try to eliminate their shadow. It is human nature to want to only project and show people the "happy" side of your-self. However, this denial or suppression festers and can manifest in destructive ways in relationships, in physical, mental, or emotional wellbeing, spiritual growth, and more. This is often seen in your self-sabotaging behavior.

Shadow work is hard and therefore many people don't want to do it. It can be ugly, uncomfortable, even painful. But doing the shadow work helps you understand yourself better, helps you communicate better, breaks destructive cycles of behavior and habits, and allows you to be more yourself. Your shadow shows you the areas you need to heal if you are willing to look at them. You have to shine light on the darkness to illuminate what needs to be healed. There are three main areas I focus on for shadow work. Self-talk, self-sabotaging, and triggers.

Self-talk are the things you tell yourself, often unknowingly, throughout the day. It is most often negative, self-limiting, and deprecating because it is a tool for your ego to keep you safe. Self-talk becomes white noise because it has been happening for so long that you might not even know you are doing it. As with any first step, we need to bring awareness to it. Become the observer. The next time you are getting ready for work, a date, or even a get-together with friends or family, pay attention to what you are saying in your head. Are you saying things like "I hate my hair," "I need to lose weight," "I swear I have more wrinkles than yesterday?" What are the thoughts running through your mind about your day? Do you say things like, "Ugh, I have that meeting with Tom today and I already know it is going to be a whole thing?" Or perhaps, "I hate family events. I know Kerry is going to get drunk. My brother isn't going to watch his kids and they are going to get out of control. I know there is going to be some family drama. There always is?"

Self-sabotaging is all about your ego trying to keep you safe. It perceives the behavior you are trying to change as the thing that keeps you alive. Of course you are having a hell of a time trying to change that behavior. A common one is weight loss. You say you are going to lose weight, put together a workout schedule, a meal plan, even reach out for an accountability buddy. But three weeks in, you don't want to work out, you are tired of eating the same foods, and you are avoiding your accountability buddy like the plague. What's that about? Don't you want to lose weight? It seemed like you did. But so did you the last ten times you set out to drop some pounds.

Triggers are the strong physical, emotional, and intellectual reactions we have to people or situations. It is that instant rage reaction when you get cut off on your way to work. The frustrations of walking down the stairs after cleaning the house to see your partner tossed their clothes on the couch when they got home from work. It's when you can feel your blood pressure rising when you're running late, and the kids still haven't rolled out of bed and you are their ride to school. That feeling of not doing anything "right" when your partner points out that you missed a spot when mowing the lawn. The way your parents make your adult-self feel like the judged teenager when they ask about your kids, work, or your partner in "that tone." Can you feel it?

These are three areas to help you connect with your shadow to bring healing and integration. To help you see through the programming and conditioning so that you can connect with your true self. Dig in and get curious about what you are saying and doing and why, free from censorship, lying, and judgments. I provide exercises at the end of this chapter for you to explore, heal, and integrate your shadow.

ILLUSION OF CONTROL

We have been conditioned to believe we can and should control anything and everything in our world. This includes the people and the situations around us. And when things begin to feel out of control, we dig our feet in, we try harder, we use our grit to get a handle on the situation. But control is simply an illusion. We have extraordinarily little control in life. That is a frightening and freeing concept.

Byron Katie, creator of The Work, international

speaker and bestselling author of several books including *Loving What Is,* said it best: "There are only three kinds of business in the universe: mine, yours, and God's." For example, a natural disaster is God's business. Your neighbor's yard is their business. Your yard is your business. Someone in your family gets an illness, that's God's business. How your partner responds to their family drama is their business. Your thoughts, feelings, actions, and reactions to how your partner brings that into your relationship is your business. As Byron Katie states often, being in your business is a full-time job.

People don't focus on their business because that is the hard work. It is so much easier to judge and try to control other people's business than it is to try to control our own. We've proven this to ourselves time and time again by trying to change our habits and behaviors without success. We naturally gravitate toward changing others, subconsciously and unconsciously. But a spiritual awakening is all about your work. Your business. No one else's.

It is widely accepted in spiritual and behavioral science circles that our thoughts create our feelings, our feelings create our actions and reactions, and those actions and reactions create our reality. Truncating this, your thoughts create your reality. Additionally, your brain is wired to find the evidence to support your belief, even if that belief is misguided. You create a negative reality when you focus on the negative. You create a positive reality when you focus on the positive. You will fail if you believe you will fail. You will succeed if you believe you will succeed. Your brain will find or create the evidence to confirm, support, and reinforce what ever belief you have. This is why creating cognitive dissonance, or a contradictory idea, belief or value, is essential in creating change.

I encourage you to get curious about how your self-talk, self-sabotage, triggers, and how your thoughts create your reality. Challenge your beliefs, ideas, and behaviors. Be open to new, contradictory evidence. Use the same rules as discussed above (no censoring, be honest, no judgment). Let me demonstrate this with a client story.

STAYING IN IT FOR THE KIDS

I had a client, Claire, who was getting pressure from her family to stay in a marriage that she knew was over. Her family told her to stay in the marriage for the kids. To ignore all the things "wrong" in the marriage and focus on "what is best for the kids." She was angry, frustrated, and questioning whether she was making the best decision for herself. I walked her through the trigger exercise I provide at the end of this chapter to see what was going on. Below is the synopsis of the exercise:

What are you reacting to? My controlling family.

They tell me to stay in a marriage even though I'm miserable and the environment is toxic for all of us. How can they tell me stay for the kids? This can't be good for them either when we're yelling and fighting all the time.

When have you felt this way before? I feel like I've been told what to do all my life. Whether as a child at home or even now with my husband. I'm always being told what to do and that what I want to do is the wrong choice.

Who else have you seen behave this way? Most of the women in my immediate family are controlling in some way, shape, or form.

How did the behavior make you feel? It made me feel like those telling me how to live my life didn't trust me, believe in me, or respect me. Like my feelings don't matter. I felt oppressed and suffocated. It makes me not trust myself either. I'm constantly second-guessing myself.

When have you behaved this way? I guess I do this with my husband. I told him everything he was doing wrong, what he "should" be doing and how he "should" be doing it. Everything from how he planned our anniversary, how he helped clean the house, to what he should say to his mom who was way too involved with his life. Whoa. I didn't realize how much I try to control him.

What does this behavior give you or protect you from? This behavior was a way for me to get what I wanted, especially when I felt alone or insecure. It was a way for me to temporarily get my needs met. It would work for a short time and then he'd revert to his usual behavior and the cycle would start all over again. I guess I was trying to protect myself from getting divorced.

Can you appreciate the value this behavior has offered you? I guess so. I stood up for my needs, even though it was not in the best way. I thought I was trying to save my marriage by telling him what to do or how to do it. But it just added to the dysfunction. I don't want to add to that.

What changes if you get conscious of this pattern? It made me realize I'm doing the same thing as my family. I don't like that. This gives me an opportunity to change it. It also makes me realize where my family is coming from so I can hear it more compassionately and not let it get to me as much. We are all coming from a place of love, even though we are not communicating it that way.

Claire and I worked on deep healing to understand these behaviors and beliefs, to connect her with herself and let go of who she thought she "should" be. Becoming aware of our thoughts, behaviors, and patterns takes work and practice. It isn't an overnight journey. It can take a lifetime to master and a good support team to help you when the ego is trying to keep you "safe." The more you practice, the freer you become from your triggers and your ego, the closer you get to your true self.

YOUR HEALING WORK

As you can start to see already, there are a lot of things coming to light that may be hard and painful to acknowledge and process. The integration of the shadow comes through the healing work you'll do around what becomes illuminated. Your mental, emotional, physical, and spiritual state will be negatively impacted if you don't do the work to heal from the things that are coming up. Some healing can be done on your own while some bigger wounds may call for coaches, therapists, or traditional or non-traditional healing support. Whatever you need is right for you. There is no shame in getting the right support and help for yourself. As a coach and an energy healer myself, there are times that I refer my clients to other holistic, medical, or behavioral professionals.

I think everyone can benefit from having a coach, a therapist, and a medical doctor on their team. My job as a coach and energy healer is to create the healing space for you to talk through and process whatever comes up, and to co-create a plan to help you move forward. The biggest, but not sole, difference between a therapist and a coach is that I, as a coach, focus on the present and the future. We may dip into the past to understand how it impacts you now. But a therapist is best suited to work with you on past issues and trauma, psychological diagnosis, and treatment.

It is also important to understand that the healing and integration process is a spiral. As you continue your shadow work and spiritual growth, there will be situations that come up several times to be witnessed, healed, and integrated at a new level. Situations that you've processed and feel like you've healed from will come back once you are ready to see the situation in a new light or from a different angle. Things that you thought you worked through years or even decades ago may come back if there is more for you to learn from it. How your healing journey happens and in whatever timeline it happens is perfect and normal for you.

FACES OF ANGUISH

Steve was a highly successful professional who was going through his spiritual awakening. He came to me because he needed support adjusting to life as he was still in the middle of his spiritual awakening process. His wife and mother-in-law both had cancer and he was taking care of them. His adult daughter came home to stay with them while she figured some things out. He led a company. He felt like he had the weight of the world on his shoulders. He was positive, optimistic, and grateful for his life. But he was feeling lost, confused, and alone because he had but one friend who was going through a similar awakening. Steve was also experiencing a physical manifestation of his ignored shadow. He was having severe back pain for which his doctor could find no medical reason. The more he tried to control the situations that were "their business" and the less he focused on "his business," the worse the pain got.

Steve was a fairly traditional man, but he was starting to see how magical the world can be, so he was open to an energy healing session with me. This was his first experience with anything like this, so I walked him through picking out crystals to be placed on him during the session and the meanings behind those that he chose. I let him know how the session would go. I use a combination of Reiki, sound healing, and shamanic techniques. During sessions I get images, sounds, feelings, and physical sensations that provide me with information about what is happening with the person on the table. I saw Steve in the dark abyss with his face contorting in what I later explained to him as faces of anguish. My throat also became tight and I started coughing. This is my sign that his throat chakra, the energy center for communication and manifestation, was blocked. As I shared these things with Steve after his session, he simply said he wasn't sure and needed to think about it.

We later had a coaching session during which he was able to express how he was feeling the weight of the world on his shoulders, that he didn't feel he had the support he needed, nor did he feel like he had the right to share his feelings with the people in his life because they relied on him and had so much going on themselves. He shared that he was also working with a meditation teacher who helped him connect with the faces of anguish, his pain, that I connected with during our energy healing session. Steve later adopted a mantra of surrender and trust to the Divine, which helped his physical symptoms subside. He later shared how everything improved as he stopped forcing and started allowing. He was becoming a believer in the counterculture approaches to life as he saw the outcomes of these approaches first-hand.

FORGIVENESS

Forgiveness is one of the most powerful tools in the healing toolkit. It is also one of the most difficult things for humans to do because of the misconceptions of what forgiveness is. Many of us think that forgiveness means forgetting about or excusing the behaviors and transgressions of the other person or people. Let's set the record straight right now.

Forgiveness is not about forgetting or excusing the behavior, transgression, or situation. Forgiveness is about releasing yourself of the story, the thoughts, feelings, and actions, that hold you hostage to the suffering caused by the situation. Let me say this another way. Forgiveness isn't about the other person or situation. It is about you. It is about loving yourself so that you can let go and move on from the pain and resentment to make room for the things that bring you love and joy in your life. Colette Baron-Read, internationally acclaimed spiritual medium, Oracle expert, and best-selling author of books and Oracle decks, said that resentment is like drinking poison and expecting the other person to get sick. To forgive is to be free of the darkness that you are choosing to hold yourself in. You don't ever have to forget. But to forgive is to heal and let go of the pain and suffering. This includes forgiving yourself.

Whether you know it or not, you are holding on to a whole host of transgressions against yourself and others that keep you in a state of fear, limitation, and self-loathing. Perhaps you told a kid on the playground they were ugly. Maybe you cheated on a test or a former lover. Maybe you stole from someone close to you or someone you didn't know. Maybe you talked shit about people in your life that you later understood differently. Maybe you can't have children the old-fashioned way because of the way you mistreated your body when you were younger. Maybe you blame yourself for not sticking up for yourself when you were abused, cheated on, assaulted or raped. What are the things you have not forgiven yourself for? Now is the time to forgive yourself.

SHADOW WORK TOOLS

You know by now that I love self-reflection and writing to gain clarity and process thoughts, feelings, emotions, and behaviors. I believe the only way to get to the other side is to move through whatever you are dealing with. To feel into the feelings and not to run away. The same rules apply; no censoring, be honest, no judgments. Remember, this is a journey and a process. There is no quick fix to thoughts, feelings, and behaviors that we've had for a long time. We have to get uncomfortable to grow, so let's get uncomfortable.

SELF-TALK EXERCISE:

For the next two days, document what you tell yourself. No additional commentary needed. Just document. Day three, review what you wrote and reflect on what you discover by answering the below.

1. What feelings come up as you read what you told yourself?
2. Why are those feeling coming up?

3. If you want to change any other self-talk
    scripts, which ones and what do you want
    to replace them with?

Now practice. Every time those thoughts that you
want to change come up, tell yourself something
like, "Thanks ego. I appreciate that you are trying to
keep me safe. But I am safe." Then, state the new
thought that you'd like to replace it with. Be realis-
tic. Don't go from, "I hate my body," to "I love my
body," if that isn't the truth. Perhaps you simply say,
"I have a body." Or start small like I did and find one
thing about your body that you do love. I said, "I
love my ankles." I focused on that for months, slowly
adding another thing I loved until now when I can
honestly say, "I love my body." Flaws and all.

SELF-SABOTAGING EXERCISE:

Think of a recent situation in which you self-sabo-
taged, and ask yourself the following:

1. What were your thoughts about the
    situation?
2. How did those thoughts make you feel?
3. How did you act or react when you felt
    that way?
4. What was the outcome when you acted or
    reacted that way?

5. Did the outcome reinforce your original thought? (Hint: It pretty much always does.)

Now flip it around.

1. What is a more positive or neutral thought about the situation?
2. How does that more positive or neutral thought make you feel?
3. How might you act or react with that new feeling?
4. What might be the outcome if you act or react in the new way?
5. Might that new outcome reinforce your more positive or neutral thought?

Here again you will want to practice this as new situations come up. It isn't important to go from an extremely negative thought to an extremely positive thought. Try to get to neutral in those situations. For example, if your initial thought is that you will never find "the one," a neutral thought to replace it with is that you will meet new people.

TRIGGERS EXERCISE

Think of a recent triggering event and write out the answers to the below questions to help you understand and clear your triggers (if you choose to):

1. What are you reacting to (what is the trigger)?
2. When have you felt this way before?
3. Who else have you seen behave this way?
4. How did this behavior make you feel?
5. When have you behaved this way?
6. What does the behavior give you or protect you from?
7. Can you appreciate the value this behavior has offered you?
8. What changes if you get conscious of this pattern?

Remember, the choice to change is yours. You can change the situation, your thought about the situation, or choose to continue to accept the suffering that it is bringing you. The choice is yours. And don't forget to practice.

FORGIVENESS EXERCISE

Remember a time or situation that you are still holding onto. This could be something your parent, partner, or stranger did to you. This could be something that you did to yourself.

1. What is the situation?
2. How do you feel about this situation?
3. How do these feelings impact your life?
4. How does holding on the feelings about the situation help you?
5. How does it hurt you?
6. What reasons do you have to hold onto this feeling?
7. What reasons do you have to let go of these feelings?
8. What do you want to do with these feelings?

Then decide and act. If you choose to hold onto the feeling, understand why and accept that you will continue to be impacted in the way you've identified in question three. You can use any other the exercises above to continue processing any associated thoughts and feelings that come up.

RELEASING RITUAL

My favorite way to release the things that no longer serve me is through a simple release ritual. Some people do this on the full moon, some on the new moon, but I say do it whenever you feel like it. You'll need pen, paper, a match or lighter, a safe receptacle to burn paper in, water (safety precaution), and an outdoor space. Write on the paper everything about the thought, behavior, feelings, or situation that you are ready to release. In your words, say to yourself or out loud something to the effect of, "Divine, I am ready to lovingly release the thoughts, feelings, and pain of this situation for my highest and greatest good. Please support me in letting go of that which no longer serves me. And so it is." Then light the piece of paper on fire and place it in the fireproof receptacle like a metal bowl, pan, or grill. Keep water nearby just in case the wind gusts and you need to put it out. Once the paper is a pile of ashes and the receptacle is cool to the touch, find a place in your yard that you can bury the ashes. I love to bury them in my garden. This ritual is a physical and symbolic way to let your mind, body, and spirit know that you are ready to let go of the situation.

APPRECIATE YOURSELF

You've been getting clear about what you think, feel, believe, and do and are starting to understand why. You've got tools to help you connect with and integrate your shadow. You've processed, healed, and released some of the things that no longer serve you so that you can make space for the things that do. These tools and practices help you clear away the fog so you can become who you were always meant to be.

Before we move on, I want you to take a minute to celebrate all the work you've just done. Thank yourself for taking the time to do the deep reflection, processing, and letting go that will bring you closer to the life you want. Be sure to get lots of rest tonight, take a salt bath, treat yourself to a beautiful, healthful dinner, and take some time to appreciate how incredible you are. It takes a strong, courageous person to dedicate themselves to doing their work. I'm so proud of you.

Now, you've already done a lot of work, but the journey has only begun. So let's continue on the adventure of spiritual awakening.

6

THE BECOMING

"Whatever is bringing you down, get rid of it. Because you'll find that when you're free...your true self comes out."

— TINA TURNER

Shortly after my spiritual awakening crumbling, I was slapped with realization that much of my life wasn't working for me. I felt empty, unfulfilled, numbed, and had an overwhelming feeling that it was time to change. Though I didn't know what changes to make, when, and how. It was also terrifying to think I wanted to "blow up" my life. I bet you feel much the same way.

To support you, this chapter is dedicated to helping you reconnect with your true self so you can decide what you want less or more of and bring you closer to an intentional, fulfilling life. You'll learn about the role that your expectations and the expectations of others play in your life and decision making. You'll understand the potential changes to your personal and professional relationships and situations that may take place as you step more fully into your true self, and the power of letting go as change happens. You'll also do one of my favorite exercises, the joy inventory, which will help you reconnect with the things that light you up.

THE ONLY CONSTANT IS CHANGE

The people I've worked with that have gone through a spiritual awakening also feel that they need to make drastic changes to their life after they deprogram and decondition themselves. They realize that that job they are in is what their parents wanted for them or that they fell into it. They realize their romantic relationships have been on autopilot and they no longer know the people they share homes with let alone if they want to be with those people anymore. They realize they are self-medicating in one way or another and decide to quit drinking, quit smoking, stop working so many hours, stop taking so many classes, or stop whatever self-medicating behavior they have – usually cold turkey. They may change their eating habits because they don't like meat or realize they are vegetarian because their parents were. They realize they don't like country music but listen to it because that's what they were raised around. Or they may be surprised to find out they have biases toward different races, genders, the LGBTQ+ community, or other marginalized groups that they didn't know they had. If you are experiencing any of this, know that it is perfectly normal and okay. As Maya Angelou once told Oprah, "When you know better, you do better." Once you bring awareness to the "thing" that was lurking in your subconscious shadow, you can make the changes you want.

The spiritual awakening process allows you to live an intentional life. Living an intentional life takes awareness, vigilance, practice, patience, and compassion. You might be thinking I sound like a broken record, and I am. I'm using repetition in this book to help you build strong neural pathways for a new way of thinking and behaving. To disrupt your old ways of being. We touched on this a bit in Chapter 4 when talking about the programming and conditioning that takes place from family, friends, media, and society. We want to disrupt the ego so we can affect your conscious and subconscious behavior. Remember? Science.

BINDING EXPECTATIONS

Expectations are another shackle keeping you in your programmed state, prohibiting you from stepping into who you are meant to be. Letting go of your expectations or yourself and the expectations that others put on you can be one of the hardest things to let go of because you identify with them. At work you are the hardest worker in your department. You are the attentive partner at home. You are the one that everyone leans on for support because you are their rock. You are a high achiever, always striving to be and do better. These are just a couple of examples of how expectations are your identity.

MORTALITY AWAKENING

Sascha was another high-achieving professional. Her friends and partner brought all their problems to her to help figure out the right path forward. She had new job opportunities knocking on her door because they knew she was great at what she did. She started to have more panic attacks that seemed to come out of nowhere. She started to get more frequent migraines. But she pushed through because she needed to show up for her boss, her team, her partner, and herself. This went on for several years. Her physical symptoms worsened, but she kept pushing through, getting praise for what a trooper she was.

Not only did those around her expect her to show up despite what she was going through, but she expected this of herself, too. And then she found a lump in her breast.

Sascha suddenly realized she created a life of fulfilling everyone else's expectations and needs except her. She didn't feel she could tell anyone because she didn't want to put her perceived burden on anyone else. She couldn't take time off from work because she had so many deadlines coming up that she was expected to meet, and she didn't want to let anyone down. She didn't even tell her partner at the time because he had enough on his plate. Faced with her mortality and feeling as if she didn't have any support, she broke open.

She thought if she got the news that she had limited time left on the planet that she would quit her job, cash in her investments, and spend the rest of her days traveling around the world. Being forced to face her mortality forced her to get clear on her priorities quickly. She had to have surgery, but she was going to live. She decided after surgery that she was going to make some big changes.

Together, we created a plan that helped her decide what she wanted to do next in her career, where she wanted to live, and if her relationship was still working for her or not. Understanding what you want to change is just the beginning. Sascha faced a lot of fear, worked through a lot of programming, and worked through releasing the expectations she put on herself about who she was to other people and herself. We worked through many of the same tools already provided in this book, and we used a joy inventory list that I'll share at the end of this chapter to help her find the job and the activities in life to bring her more fulfillment.

COMING AND GOING

As I mentioned before, change is difficult for everyone even when it is for the best. This is especially true for the people who come and go throughout our lives. You will have people who don't understand what you are going through and want you to stay the same. You will have people flat-out reject the person you are becoming and tell you that you are crazy, selfish, depressed, just going through a phase, ungrateful, or a whole host of other things. I'm sure you understand why this will be hard. But please know this is normal.

As you change, your energetic vibration changes. We are all energetic beings. This isn't just a "woo-woo" concept. Science has proven that everything is made of energy vibrating at different speeds. I still remember Mr. Bowen in ninth grade physical science knocking on the desk and explaining it was simply energy vibrating so slowly that it looks and feels like a solid. Mind blown. The slower the vibration, the denser it becomes. That's why you'll also hear people say that talking about negative, heavy topics is "low vibe" and talking about happy, joyful, light topics as "high vibe." People are the same way in that we are all vibrating energy.

People with different vibrations than you will either be attracted to, neutral, or repelled by your vibration. Think of a time when you walked into a room and were instantly attracted to someone. Or when someone walked into the room and you got a "creepy vibe" from them. You were picking up on their energy and it either was or wasn't resonating with your vibration.

LET GO. SURRENDER. TRUST.

As hard as it may be, letting go of the people, places, and things that no longer resonate with you will expedite your spiritual growth. We are programmed to think we need to stay committed to our people and our jobs at all costs. But those things can be holding us back, and the work is about letting go, surrendering to the Divine, and trusting that what is ahead is for our highest and greatest good. The people, places, and things that are going away are making room for new people, places, and things that are in alignment with the new you.

Leaving my corporate job was a long, labored process. I loved my boss, my team, and I was making great money, but I didn't feel like I was contributing to the greater good. My mom was immensely proud of what I accomplished and didn't understand why I wanted to leave my successful, high paying job to become a life coach. Even more, my spiritual friends said I should stay so I can keep funding my spiritual education and travel. My partner didn't fully understand it, but he said he would support whatever I wanted to do. I created a financial plan, an exit strategy, and worked with my coach at the time to implement the exit strategy. But my ego was screaming at me that my life would be ruined by me leaving the financial security of my job. Remember, the ego comes from a place of fear and lack. And I was feeling all those things. My work became my fear. I worked with my coach to understand why the fear was there, what it was trying to tell me, and how to move through it. My ego made up all these stories to keep me in a place of fear and lack. Stories about how my partner was going to leave me because the only reason he was with me was because of my financial success. How I was going to be living on the streets because I wouldn't have my partner nor any money to pay for my own place. That once I left the world and the life I built over the last thirty-eight years, I'd never be able to go back if I decided to do so later. My ego told me that I didn't know enough, wasn't smart enough, trained enough, and skilled enough to help anyone.

I remember the day I gave notice to my boss. Remember, I loved my boss and I didn't want to let him down. I didn't want to let my team down. I had put the weight of expectations on myself. I was shaking. I may have even cried. The words fumbled out of my mouth. And the response was support, love, and acceptance. And just like that, the weight was lifted. I went up to the roof after that to calm my nerves. I looked over the Puget Sound and a wave of lightness moved throughout my body. And with that, things began moving and changing quickly. Letting go, surrendering, and trusting the Divine had my back allowed me to take a big step into my true self.

JOY INVENTORY

You will want to get clear on what brings you joy and happiness now so that you also have a better picture of what people, places, or things you are ready to let go of. As always, it is your choice if or when you want to make any changes. Please use the three rules of no censorship, complete honesty, and no judgment. Grab your journal and a pen and go somewhere you won't be distracted for a while.

First, I want you to connect with your five-year-old-self. I want you to close your eyes after you read the following and step back in time to when you were five. Feel into it. Picture what you wore, what your home looked like, what your haircut looked like. I was rocking a sweet eighties bowl cut at five. Adorable, right? Okay, back to you. What was your favorite food? Your favorite toy? What games did you love to play? Did you enjoy playing outside in the woods like me? Did you like to play with dolls or action figures? Did you draw, paint, or play with play-dough? Did you love dress-up and make-believe? What activities brought you the most joy and happiness? After you feel like you can hear, taste, touch the memories of you at age five, write down some of those things that come to mind. Still connected to your five-year-old self, what did you want to be when you grew up? Write that down. I wanted to be a bunny. Not even kidding. I've always believed in magic.

Next, we're going to fast forward a bit. But not too far. Imagine your sixteen-year-old self. At sixteen, we've lived some. We've had some experiences that shape our thoughts and expectations of what life will be like once we're an adult. If it helps get into your sixteen-year-old self, remember what you dressed like, what your hair was like. Remember who you hung out with, where you hung out, what you did when you were together. How would your friends describe you back then? What activities brought you joy and happiness at sixteen? Did you write or play music? Were you in theater? Did you enjoy babysitting? Playing ball? Going to shows or the movies? Camping? Debate? Write down the things that brought you the most happiness and joy. At sixteen, what did you want to do when "you grew up"? Not what you thought you should do, but what you genuinely wanted to do? Is it different or the same as when you were five? Is it different or the same as what you do now?

Now, step into the present moment. What are the things that you do today that bring you the most joy and fulfillment? This is not the time to write down what you think you "should" write down. No one else will read this, no one will judge you. Don't feel bad if you are having a hard time finding an answer, or don't feel bad if the things that do bring you the most joy and fulfillment aren't what you "think" it should be. Looking at your job and your career, where are you fulfilled and what might it be missing? Reflecting on your relationships. Are you getting the love, support, affection, acceptance, and support you want? What are you missing in your relationships right now? Write it down.

Lastly, fast forward to your eighty-year-old self. I want you to write a letter from your eighty-year-old self to who you are now. Project yourself into the future and imagine all that you have done, who you have become, what you are excited about. Where do you live at eighty? What do you enjoy doing at eighty? Who do you surround yourself with? Once you have this image, write yourself a letter. Share what you've accomplished, what you are proud of, what brought you the most happiness, joy, and fulfillment. What advice does your eighty-year-old-self have for you?

BRINGING IT ALL TOGETHER

We've covered a lot of ground in this chapter. You've decided what you want less or more of in your life, you now understand the constraints of expectations, you have an idea of the potential changes ahead, and you completed the joy inventory exercise. Now you'll put it all together.

I want you to put these four writing exercises away for one week. After a week, read through them again and identify any trends between them. What surprised you? What of these things that bring you joy are in your life now? What things might you want to make room for? What things do you want to let go of to make room for the things that bring you more joy? Write down the answers in your journal.

I encourage you to start by incorporating one thing that you want to add into your week and removing one thing that you want to let go of. As always, the choice is yours. You've brought aware-ness to things that bring you joy, happiness, and fulfillment. It is your choice to change things, change your mind about things, or accept things as they are? Whatever you choose, the choice brings you one step closer to your authentic self and a life well-lived.

7

RESISTANCE IS FUTILE

"Every time you are tempted to react in the same old way, ask if you want to be a prisoner of the past or a pioneer of the future."

— DEEPAK CHOPRA

Resistance will become a close friend as you adjust to life after your spiritual awakening. This chapter is designed to help you work through resistance to change that you will feel and face from those around you and your-self. I'll review examples of resistance that may come up and the tips and tools to work through it in this chapter. I'll spend some time on self-care, and I'll share some helpful breathwork exercises to help move through feelings that come up. You'll finish this chapter with reflection journaling and a self-care exercise.

THE BIRTHPLACE OF RESISTANCE

Resistance is a natural response to change. Your ego, which runs the show most of the time, is here to keep you alive and safe, but it keeps you blind by reminding you of the fear and lack of "enough" (not good enough, smart enough, worthy enough, etc.) that you possess. It keeps you safe by whispering self-limiting beliefs and catastrophic stories to keep you frozen or fighting and running from the change. And then there is the resistance from everyone else.

The people in your life expect you to act, react, and move through life in a specific way based on how you have moved through life so far. They have expectations of you based on your conditioning and programming from family, friends, and society that impact you on both a conscious and subconscious level. It's no wonder you'd face resistance to anything new when your inner and outer world wants to keep you in the box you've been filling for so long.

In order to make changes to things that are so deeply rooted in you, you have to be cracked open so that you can see that there is a different way of life; a life that can be intentional and well-lived, full of joy and happiness. Can you imagine it? What would that look like? What would that feel like? The more that you work through your thoughts, beliefs, and behaviors, the more that you let go, surrender, and trust that the Divine supports you, the closer you can be to that life that you know you are meant to live. The more you practice the tools and techniques provided in this book, the closer you become to your true self. But then, you get knocked down again.

It is inevitable that something is going to happen that tries to pull you back into old habits, thoughts, and stories tied to who you were before your spiritual awakening. You are going to hit points where you feel stuck. You are going to face resistance from family, friends, society, and yourself. You are going to feel frustrated that you have grown so much and are suddenly reverting to old ways of being. This is a sign that you are about to go through another spiritual growth spurt.

REMEMBER THE BASICS

When you get hit with resistance and fall back into old habits, go back to the basics. Refer back to chapters that cover the thoughts, feelings, or behavioral tools that are relevant to your situation. Get curious about what is going on and why. Be patient, loving, and compassionate to yourself. Take it one day at a time. Don't worry about where you want to go or how you want to get there. Use this as a time to go deeper and be open to the process as it unfolds. Remember, you are exactly where you need to be right now.

Remember that the ego is trying to keep you safe. Egoic resistance can sound like real, logical, tangible reasons why you can't do something. Use one of the techniques from Chapter 4 to investigate what is coming up and why. Ask yourself what your ego is trying to protect you from and why. Ask yourself what falling back into old habits would give you and your ego. What would it cost you? Be patient and kind to yourself. Be open, honest, and leave judgments at the door.

PERSISTENCE THROUGH RESISTANCE

As you continue to integrate your new thoughts, feelings, beliefs, and behaviors after a spiritual awakening, you will face polarizing resistance. It often represents two competing thoughts or feelings and is shrouded by the stories we tell ourselves about these thoughts or feelings. These stories then make it hard for you fully get behind either option and keep you stuck. You may want freedom to be your own boss, but you want the security of a regular paycheck. You may want to end your unfulfilling relationship, but you don't know if anyone else will love you. You may want to go to Bali for an incredible, potentially life-changing retreat, but you feel like you are behind on your retirement savings and want to put more money toward that.

RESISTANCE FROM THOSE WE LOVE

Your family and friends love you and want the best for you. But even knowing this, they usually don't want you to change. They are comfortable with who you are and your relationship with them. They rely on you to play a specific role in their lives. It makes them uncomfortable when you start to change and adjust to life after your spiritual awakening because it forces them to look at themselves.

As humans, we often want to share our lives with those we love, and I'm going to guess you are the same. You want to share what is going on with you, what you are learning and experiencing. But often your loved ones will get triggered by your changes and are unable to support our growth. For example, when I quit drinking, the people around me suddenly felt like they needed to justify how much and how often they drank. I told them it was just a thirty-day experiment to get back in touch with myself, but they were often triggered by this and felt that they needed to evaluate their own drinking because I was.

A client of mine was moving out of state to live in a place that she felt resonated with her soul more. Her mom's response was, "I thought you wanted to have kids," as if the place she was moving to didn't allow kids. Another client left her well-paying corporate sales job to start a Reiki practice because she wanted to help people instead of "sell stuff." Her mom asked her if this was just a break and when did she think she'd get another corporate job. All well-meaning loved ones who didn't understand why these individuals would go against the grain and live a life that didn't match what they wanted for them.

A RESISTANCE STORY

Charlie was living across the country from his family with his partner for the past few years. He was feeling a strong need to move home to help with some family issues, but he also wanted to keep advancing in his career. He was facing the decision of stepping back into who he was in his home state or moving forward with who he was becoming. Charlie was experiencing inner turmoil. Should he move home and embrace the blue-collar, family-oriented man that was happy with having beers with the neighbors in the garage? He always thought that was who he was, and it is who his family wanted him to be. Or should he stay where he was, continue to climb the corporate ladder, and enjoy the opportunities and experiences that he had grown accustomed to and valued?

Charlie decided to move home. He opted for

what was comfortable and known instead of moving past the fear of the unknown. He quickly realized he had made a mistake. He realized he no longer had much in common with the people he grew up with. He didn't like his new job, and had a hard time connecting with the people he worked with. He also realized that he couldn't help his family figure out their issues and recognized that his family dynamics were causing damage to his relationship with his partner. That's when we started to work together to help him work through his resistance.

I worked with Charlie to help him identify the competing parts, voices, and stories related to the situation, and which were from him and which were from his family. We got clear on what each part and voice wanted and needed for Charlie. Some voices wanted safety, security, and control, while others wanted freedom, love, and acceptance. I helped him understand what these competing thoughts needed. Some parts needed to be heard, some felt, some understood, others respected, and some parts just need to be seen. We then integrated the parts, created peace of mind, and decided what Charlie wanted to do next.

Charlie was able to move past the resistance and fear and let go of the person he and his family thought he was so he could step into who he is. He was a corporate person and loved the challenge of corporate life. He moved back across the country with his partner and things started aligning in his life like never before. He is in a job he loves with people he highly respects. He set healthy boundaries with his family that allows him to still be involved with much less stress and frustration. Charlie continues to do his growth work and is building a stronger relationship with his partner.

BOUNDARIES

I've talked about boundaries a few times in this book, so let me define it. Boundaries are the guidelines or rules that you put in place to create a safe, healthy, and happy relationship with yourself and others. Boundaries can trigger a lot of emotions for people such as rejection, limitation, exclusion, being left out, etc. Boundaries don't mean walls. They mean setting yourself or a relationship up for success by being clear about what you will or won't deal with so that you can make sure that you are getting what you need and want. You can set boundaries around people, situations, and yourself. That can include the amount of time you spend with someone or something (such as work hours), the types of conversations you have, the activities you participate in, the type of touch or affection that feels safe for you, or the amount of alone time you have. There are lots of different boundaries that can support you on your personal and spiritual growth journey.

Setting new boundaries with people that you've had long-standing relationships with takes compassion, open communication, and practice. You are the only one responsible for creating, communicating, and maintaining your boundaries. I say this because I have seen too many times that someone decides to put a boundary in place but doesn't communicate it, allows the boundary to be breached, or puts themselves back into the situation they were trying to put a boundary around and then plays the victim when the other person wasn't respecting their boundary.

When setting boundaries, you must be willing to uphold your boundaries and decide what you will do if the other person is not honoring them. That may mean limiting interaction with the people, places, or things that are not supporting your highest good. It could mean saying goodbye to relationships that are toxic, even when they are family. I know how hard that is, but sometimes it is the best thing for you when others aren't honoring and respecting the boundaries you put in place. Again, it is your responsibility to create and maintain the boundaries that keep you feeling safe, healthy, and happy.

SELF-CARE 101

Self-care is usually the last thing on most people's mind. I talk a lot of self-care with my clients because it is a key to unlock your potential and personal power. We spend so much of our life giving our time, energy, and self to those around us, and we end up giving everything and having nothing left for ourselves. Adjusting to life after a spiritual awakening calls for next-level self-care.

I often share the concept of the glass half full. This is not an original. I heard it a few years back and it resonated with me, and I still use it today. The cup half full concept is about having enough in your own cup for yourself and others. If your glass is already half empty, and your partner boss comes along and "takes a drink" by asking you to pick up the dry cleaning on the way home, you now have less in your cup. Then your friend calls you about a situation that may impact their entire world and takes "two big gulps" from your glass. The day isn't even over, and your glass is almost empty. Then you get home from a long day and the kids ask what's for dinner. But your glass is now empty, and you yell, "I can't make one more decision today."

When your glass is empty, you have no more energy for yourself or anyone else. If you get thirsty later, tough. If someone else is thirsty, tough for them too. There's nothing left. Now you're left dehydrated, weak, angry, and if one more person asks you for something, you might just smash the glass on the ground. Suddenly you change from being the person who others count on to the unreliable person because you have no more to give. But what happens if you take the time to fill yourself up?

Taking care of yourself is how you keep your glass full. It means connecting with your natural rhythm, your mind, body, and spirit to listen to the messages it is giving you. It is telling you all the time what it needs. You just need to get quiet enough to listen. Instead of dashing from one activity to the next, from meeting to meeting, from home to work and back, rarely stopping for a bite to eat or a bathroom break, you slow down. You start paying attention to the way your body communicates what it needs. It tells you this with aches, pain, and disease. The reoccurring headaches, back pain, random chest or stomach pains, heart palpitations, insomnia, or auto-immune disorders, physical issues that the doctors can't find a medical cause for (remember Steve and his back?). These are all ways that your body is asking you for something.

By slowing down and paying attention to what your mind, body, and spirit need, you'll be able to take better care of yourself. When you take better care of yourself, you'll notice more energy, more mental clarity, less stress, more resilience, more effective decision-making, creativity, and you'll be able to connect with your natural intuition.

There are many ways to take care of yourself. Get that massage that you keep putting off (which reminds me...), read that book you've been excited to get into, go for a hike in the woods to reconnect with nature. If you want to include others, you can go out for a lovely dinner, get a coffee, tea, or beverages with friends, or join a club or group that focuses on something from your joy inventory list. If time and money are concerns, you can take a walk around the block, use a breathing technique, or do a quick meditation. There is no excuse to not take care of yourself.

BREATHWORK

Breathing is a quick way to slow it all down and listen to your body instead of the rat race mind, which is incredibly helpful when you are working through resistance and fear. It may sound too simple to be true, but it is profoundly effective. It can be done anytime, anywhere, and you only need a few minutes. I often start my coaching sessions with a breathing exercise, and my clients love how it helps them clear their minds, calms them down, and makes them feel more peaceful.

Breathing techniques and practices are found in many spiritual traditions. They are widely used to help calm the nervous system, reduce stress, anxiety, slow the mind chatter, and even connect with Spirit. Below are three breathing techniques that I use and use with my clients. Try each one out a few times and decide which work best for you when you are in a heightened state of resistance or stress and you want to slow down.

Let's start with a wave breath. You can lie down with your arms at your side, palms facing up, or sitting with a straight but soft spine, feet flat on the floor and your hands in your lap with palms up. Your eyes can be closed or open. Relax your jaw, allowing your mouth to open slightly with the tip of your tongue touching the roof of your mouth. Inhale through your nose to the count of five and exhale out through your mouth to the count of five, constricting your throat slightly so the breath sounds like an ocean wave. Continue your wave breath for one to five minutes.

Next is the four-seven-eight breath. This technique has its roots in yoga's pranayama. You can lie down with your arms at your side, palms facing up, or sitting with a straight but soft spine, feet flat on the floor and your hands in your lap with palms up. Your eyes can be closed or open. Relax your jaw allowing your mouth to open slightly with the tip of your tongue touching the roof of your mouth. Close your mouth to inhale to the count of four. Hold your breath for a count of seven. Then open your mouth slightly again and exhale to the count of eight. Repeat four to eight times.

The last breathing exercise I'll share with you is the box breath. This is one that my Shamanic teacher and mentor, don Oscar Miro-Quesada, often uses in his work. It helps clear the mind, relaxes the body, and improves focus. Great for shamanic journeying. You can lie down with your arms at your side, palms facing up, or sitting with a straight but soft spine, feet flat on the floor and your hands in your lap with palms up. Your eyes can be closed or open. Relax your jaw allowing your mouth to open slightly with the tip of your tongue touching the roof of your mouth. Close your mouth to inhale to the count of four. Hold your breath at the top for a count of four. Open your mouth slightly again and exhale to the count of four. Then hold at the bottom for a count of four. Repeat at least four times or continue until you feel a sense of calm wash over you.

NO JOURNALING?

Of course, we have a journaling exercise. I want you to journal about what resistance is coming up for you. Explore the resistance by asking where it is coming from and why. Use your five whys technique to get to the root of it and explore how you want to change it. Use your breathing techniques when you feel stressed and practice radical self-care are you are working through the resistance that comes up for you. Pick one thing that you will do for your self-care this week, and journal about the experience. Did you feel resistant to doing it? If so, why? If you enjoyed it, write about what you enjoyed and how you will incorporate more of it in the future. No matter how much you try to avoid resistance, it will happen. Remember the basics of staying curious, being patient and compassionate to yourself; prioritize self-care; and use your tools and tips from this and previous chapters. These things will help you navigate the resistance with confidence and clarity.

8

INNER WISDOM

"During my life journey I've discovered an interesting thing; once you stop seeking outside, you discover what already resides within."

— RASHEED OGUNLARU

You have an incredible inner wisdom that can help guide you and makes decision making easier when we can tap into our higher self. This inner wisdom is one of the most helpful and fun to use tools that I've found on my journey. It is your intuition.

We've been taught our whole life that we need parents, teachers, mentors, or others around us to show us the way. We are told to go to others for advice and to help us solve problems. To help us make decisions. We've been told we don't possess the wisdom and the tools within us to guide us on this journey called life. But that isn't true. Sure, you need a mechanic to fix your car or a doctor to reset your bone. But when it comes to decision making and problem-solving, you have all the wisdom and know-how you need. You may need help tapping into that, to connect with and learn how to listen to your intuition. But you have everything you need within you right now.

In this chapter, I'm going to help you start to tap into your inner wisdom. You'll understand your energy and what happens when it is imbalanced. You'll learn about empathic abilities, the five clairs, intuitive development tools, manifestation, and I'll walk you through a meditation to ground and clear your energy. You'll get the opportunity for an exercise and reflection journaling focused on getting to know your inner guidance system – your intuition. We are all intuitive beings, but most of us have disconnected from our intuition. Society values logic, data, and producing over intuition, emotions, and creativity. This creates an imbalance in our masculine and feminine energy.

MASCULINE AND FEMININE ENERGY

Masculine and feminine energies have nothing to do with gender, and we all have both in us. However, due to how we were raised and how we've been conditioned, we often have an energy imbalance.

Masculine energy is what our society favors and encourages. Masculine energy is logical, analytical, productive, and a "doing" energy. It is the side of you that wants to compete, to problem solve, to push forward, to strive for bigger, better, faster, more. The side that rationalizes what is happening and puts together the pros and cons list. It is the part of you that wants to crunch numbers and make data-driven decisions. It is organized and strategic. Masculine energy is giving and is often associated with fire. It is also known as Yang.

Feminine energy is seen as less desirable in modern Western society. It is intuitive and empathetic. Creative, passionate, emotional, and sensual. Feminine energy is going with the flow and allowing. It is compassionate, gentle, and nurturing. But it can also be stormy with emotional waves. Feminine energy is receiving and associated with water. It is also known as Yin.

Being out of balance can prevent you from connecting with your Higher Self and your intuition. Finding balance can bring you wholeness and can help you access the inner wisdom to make decision making and navigating life smoother. You can recognize if you have an imbalance by observing your thoughts, feelings, and behaviors.

Having too much masculine energy can cause

burn out, anger, and frustration. You may be a workaholic and you may cause issues in otherwise healthy relationships, so you have a problem to solve. You may self-sabotage your work so you have another obstacle to overcome. Most of your decision making is based on logic and data analysis. You may be uncomfortable expressing and dealing with emotions. Having too much masculine energy can also leave you feeling anxious when things are going smoothly.

Having too much feminine energy can cause you to be an emotional mess and you can end up living your life for others, leading to bitterness and feelings of being taken for granted. You are an extreme empath, taking on and drowning in other people's emotions. Your need for solitude to manage your emotions can lead to a loss of friends and the growing feeling of abandonment. Having too much feminine energy can cause you to sacrifice your needs for the needs of others to make them feel loved, supported, and accepted. It can also lead to assumptions and making up stories in your head about a person and a situation because you don't want to rock the boat by asking for clarification.

Balanced masculine energy can help you solve complex problems and move mountains to accomplish great things. It is your ability for curiosity, learning, and adventure. You can balance your masculine energy by taking a class, starting a new hobby, learning something new, delegating tasks or projects to others and being prepared to be okay if it fails, or use that curiosity to understand your relationship with emotions.

Balanced feminine energy can help you connect with people on an emotional level to understand what they need and to create a safe space to support them. Balanced feminine energy allows you to connect with your emotions, your intuition, your creativity, and your sensuality which enables you to live an authentic life. You can balance your feminine energy by meditating, taking naps, doing a creative project, journaling, taking time for yourself, and setting boundaries so that you aren't giving too much of yourself away.

EMPATHY

Empathy is the capacity to feel someone else's emotions as if they were your own. You may have realized that you are an empath after you went through your spiritual awakening. You may have found that you suddenly feel things on a much deeper level. You may also realize that you feel things on a much broader level, like you are feeling the emotions of the world. This is where you probably realized that we are all connected. That what someone else does impacts more than them, and what you do impacts more than you. Our actions and reactions can create a ripple effect that is felt throughout the world, whether others realize it or not.

I thought it was important to cover empathy in this book because it can be overwhelming to start feeling things so deeply when you may have been disconnected from your emotions for much of your life. Empathy is a superpower. You can help people in a new way because you can feel what is underneath the words they are saying.

Everyone feels empathy in a different way. Some may feel someone's emotions as if they are their own. Others feel someone's emotions as a physical sensation. Someone may tell you that they are great, but you suddenly feel sad. Or someone said they had an amazing weekend, but you feel an ache in your stomach or a tightness in your chest. As your empathetic abilities grow, it is important to practice good energy hygiene and protect yourself from the potential overwhelm. I'll cover some tools for this at the end of this chapter.

EMPATH IN TRAINING

I always knew I was an empath. I feel things on a deep level. I have always been sensitive to loud noises and large crowds. I would often need days of solitude following the holidays or highly populated events. Friends, family, and total strangers open up to me, sharing the problems and their deepest, darkest secrets. As a young twenty-one-year-old, I'd be chatting with someone at the bar and get an overwhelming feeling or a knowing that they were in pain. One too many beers, and I'd walk up to people and ask why they were feeling a certain way. And they'd open up to me.

In my mid-twenties I went to a psychic for a reading. She picked up on my empathic abilities and asked what I was doing to cleanse and protect my energy. I had no idea what she was talking about. I didn't know what that even meant. She confirmed some of the empath symptoms and then shared with me a few techniques. Then years later, I worked with a coach who could read chakras, and she gave me more tools to help cleanse, clear, and protect my energy. I still use the techniques personally and professionally.

INTUITIVE GIFTS

As you connect with your intuition and your empathic abilities, you start to notice other gifts beginning to emerge. Some believe that our intuition is really our first sense, not our sixth. Most common intuitive abilities or senses are the five basic clairs, or "clear" intuitive senses. These can be experienced internally, similar to the imagination, or in our external physical world similar to how we experience our five senses.

Clairvoyance, or clear seeing, is seeing images in your mind's eye like a daydream. It may be a full scene, or it may just be flashes of images. For example, close your eyes and imagine a bonfire. Imagine everything from how big it is to what the flames look like. That is what clairvoyance feels like. In the case of some mediums and people who channel, you might also see images in your physical world. That has not been my experience, but I know other talented Intuitives that do see images in their physical world.

Clairaudience, or clear hearing, is when you hear words, phrases, sounds, or music in your mind's ear. For example, that fire that we were just imagining... what does it sound like? Can you hear the crackle of the burning wood? That is the most common way clairaudience is experienced. Again, some people hear a disembodied voice or sound outside of themselves.

Clairsentience, or clear feeling, is when we tune into the emotions or physical pain of those around us, which can include spirit. This is different from an empath in that a clairsentient not only feels and can absorb the emotional or physical pain, but they also get information and details about the situation such as what is causing the pain.

Clairalience, or clear smelling, is the ability to

smell odors that don't have a physical source. The smell of tobacco that your father used to smoke, the perfume that your grandmother used to wear, or the wet dog smell of your passed fur baby are all signs that your loved ones are near. I smelled my grandmother in my house the day that she died. My partner couldn't smell it, but I did, which is how I knew she was visiting me.

Clairgustance, or clear tasting, is the ability to taste something that doesn't have a physical source. Again, this is usually something that will remind us of a loved one to let you know they are near. Some intuitives say that emotions, colors, or experiences have certain tastes. They develop what different tastes mean to them over time to be able to interpret the information they get.

Claircognizance, or clear knowing, is the ability to just know something that is not common knowledge for that person. Thoughts may suddenly pop into your head out of nowhere. This one happened for me when my sister got pregnant. I just had this feeling that she was before she told the family (many moons ago).

Nurturing these intuitive gifts helps you to connect with your higher self, your spirit guides, your angels, your ancestors, other light beings that support you on your path to your highest and greatest good. They can help you tap into the Akashic Records, the non-physical, higher dimensional library that holds the records to your past, present, and future.

Gifts develop and manifest differently for each person. There is no one way to develop or experience a gift. You may find that you have one or several gifts. However they show up for you is perfect for you. Strengthening these skills can help you tap into your inner wisdom to get the guidance, clarity, and answers to navigate your life and help others if that is what you choose to do. It also is important to know that you only use these gifts with others after you get their explicit permission to do so, and your gifts are used for the highest and greatest good of all.

INTUITION DEVELOPMENT TOOLS

There are so many tools and ways to develop your intuition. I always encourage people to start with meditation first. You have to quiet the mind to "hear" your intuition. Secondly, I encourage people to use automatic writing techniques. Physically write a question at the top of a piece of paper with your dominant (writing) hand, set a timer for ten minutes, and write whatever comes out using your non-dominate hand. Keep writing until the timer goes off. Even if you just write, "I'm writing because I have to, and I hope the timer goes off soon because this sucks." Just keep writing. Creative projects, such as painting, drawing, writing, or sculpting is another great way to nurture your intuition because it connects you to your feminine energy. Once you have quieted the mind with more consistency and are feeling more adventurous, you can explore divination tools such as Tarot, Oracle cards, runes, pendulums, tea leaves, and so many other options.

OOPS! I MANIFESTED.

You'll also start to notice more synchronicities as your intuition and connection to Spirit grows and you take more steps toward your true self. Synchronicity is a concept first introduced by renowned psychologist Carl Jung. Jung defined a synchronicity as "the acausal connection of two or more psychic and physical phenomena." Said another way, synchronicities are the meaningful coincidences with no causal relationship. For example, Charlie, who you met earlier who was deciding if he should move again or not, was watching a movie called *The Wedding Year* with his partner one night after they had moved back to his home state. While the plot was about a couple's relationship being put to the test with a yearlong schedule of weddings, one of the storylines was about the leading actor facing the decision to live near his family and be who they wanted him to be or step into who he was meant to be and have a future with the leading lady. I remember Charlie saying, "Of course that was the issue in the movie. I feel like the Divine is yelling at me." Unbeknownst to Charlie, he was manifesting these synchronicities from his thoughts into his physical reality.

You, too, will start to manifest on accident. You will see how your thoughts create physical manifestation in your 3D world. You'll think of something in the morning and then later that day or week, it will magically appear. Start practicing your manifestation gifts. Try saying you want to see an elephant that day, and then let the thought go. If you try to hold onto it or be intensely looking for it, it won't show up. But when you think about it and release it, it could show up in the most delightful way. The more you practice, the more you will trust it, and the stronger your manifesting abilities will become. Remember, our thoughts create our feelings, which create our actions and reactions, which reinforce our thoughts. Our thoughts create our reality. Use your powers wisely and always for the highest and greatest good of all.

GROUNDING AND CLEARING MEDITATION

It is easy to spend too much time developing and playing with our intuition. Meditation is a great way to quiet the mind to get in touch with the body, connect with your higher self, and your inner wisdom. It has been proven to reduce stress, anxiety, and increase overall wellness. It is also important to stay grounded and balanced as you are adjusting to life after a spiritual awakening and are spending intentional time and effort to develop your intuitive gifts. You are still a human living on the 3D plane with others. You can get grounded by putting your bare feet in the grass, eating a whole, unadulterated food, or using meditation, just to name a few options. I use the following grounding and clearing meditation for myself each morning and in my coaching, energy healing, and readings.

To start, get into a comfortable position. This can be sitting or lying down, hands in your lap or at your side with palms up. Eyes closed or open. Whatever feels best for you is perfect. Breathe naturally. No need to change anything. Start by noticing the way the chair, bed, or floor supports your body. Feel how the air feels on your skin. Notice if there are any sounds around you. Bringing your awareness to your space and your body allows you to slow down the mind chatter and listen to what your body is saying to you.

Now, begin taking deep, full breaths that extend your lower belly. I call this "Buddha belly breaths." Breathe in for a count of four, hold for four, and then exhale to the count of four. Let that beautiful belly relax and extend.

Next, imagine your roots growing from the bottom of your feet. Going past the floor, the grass, the rocks, the boulders, and all the way down into mother earth. I want you to set the intention to release to Mother Earth any thoughts, feelings, emotions, or energy that isn't yours. Allow her to take that which no longer serves you and transmute it into love and light. Now imagine that beautiful, grounding, regenerative energy starts to travel up your roots. See it travel pass the boulders, the rocks, the grass, the floor, and into the soles of your feet. I want you to imagine and feel Mother Earth's red energy infusing every cell in your body. Feel it travel from your feet to your ankles, your calves, your knees. See it continue to infuse your cells as it travels up your thighs, your hips, into your stomach, swirling around your heart, up to your shoulders, down your arms, and into your hands. Imagine it continuing up your throat, into your head, and out the top of your head continuing up into the sky.

Now imagine a beautiful, golden-white light coming down from the universe, passed our sun and our moon, past the clouds, down through the roof of the building in which you are, past the ceiling in your room, and into the crown of your head. Now imagine and feel that Divine source energy infusing your cells in your head, moving to your throat, down your shoulders, arms, and hands. See the golden white light continue down your chest, swirling around your heart, continuing down your torso, into your hips, your thighs, knees, calves, ankles, feet, and continuing down your roots into Mother Earth.

Now imagine your breath flowing in and out of your heart. You can always put your hand on your heart if you have a hard time with the visualization. Once you can feel your breath going in and out of your heart, recall a person, place, or thing that bring you feelings of love, appreciation, joy, or compassion. This could be a happy childhood memory, the thought of snuggling with your babies (two-legged and four), being in nature, or being of service to people, just to name a few. Hold that feeling as you continue to breathe in and out from your heart for four more breaths.

On your next exhale, radiate the feelings of love, joy, compassion, and appreciation from your heart. Imagine these positive feelings being sent out to the universe and showering down around you. Stay with this visualization for as long as you want.

WHAT INTUITIVE GIFTS DO YOU HAVE?

Time to get out your journal again. We've covered a lot of ground in this chapter. I discussed masculine and feminine energies and what happens when they're out of balance. You learned about empathic abilities, the five clairs, intuitive development tools, manifestation, and I walked you through a meditation to ground and clear your energy. I want you to reflect and journal about how you have intentionally or unintentionally used your intuition. What do you want to develop or use more of?

I also want you to pay attention to your energy. Just for a day or two, pay attention to how your energy changes based on the people, places, or situations you experience. I want you to pay attention to how your energy is in the morning, in the middle of the day, and the evening. Do you feel full of energy or depleted? Is your mind running a mile a minute or is it peaceful? Are you feeling anxious or calm? Again, no judgment. You just want to bring awareness to how your energy fluctuates and start to understand why.

9

SOUL FAMILY

"Please remember, especially in these times of groupthink and the right-on chorus, that no person is your friend (or kin) who demands your silence or denies your right to grow and be perceived as fully blossomed as you were intended."

— ALICE WALKER

You will discover along your journey that the people who have been in your life may not be able to support you the way they have in the past. Not because they don't want to, but simply because they haven't been through a spiritual awakening or understand what you are going through. It doesn't mean they don't love you any less or that you love them any less. It simply means it is time to find your soul family. The group of people who can support you in the way that you need now and as you continue to grow and transform.

Spiritual awakening is just the first step in a life-long journey to become the fullest expression of yourself. To step into the wholeness of your gifts and your divine destiny, it requires different people at different times as you are un-becoming, healing, becoming, and continuing to grow. You may find that you need tough love at one point and a more compassionate approach to support as you find more balance in your energy.

Give yourself permission to find the right people for you and permission to let go of the people with whom you no longer resonate. You may find that some people naturally come and go, while others, usually those we have created a deep bond with, are harder to let go of. You may feel that you owe them to maintain a relationship long after the relationship became hurtful or brought you suffering. Give your-self permission to release the contract you have in your heart so both you and the other person can grieve, heal, and find freedom in new relationships that are more aligned with yourselves.

WHEN THE STUDENT IS READY, THE TEACHER WILL APPEAR... OR SOMETHING LIKE THAT

Finding the right teacher, mentor, or coach may be the first thing that you want to do. What some people don't realize is that this can come in many forms. It can be a book, a group that you find, music and art class, your higher self, spirit guides that you connect with in dreams or meditation, or any number of untraditional ways. It can also be a traditional spiritual teacher, a life coach, or a mentor with a spirituality focus.

I remember when I was early in my journey, I asked for a teacher every night. I even reached out to some spiritual teachers and kept getting denied because they were too busy. One morning, right before I woke up, one of my spirit guides who I met during a plant ceremony when I was seventeen appeared to me in my dream. She hugged me and said, "You have everything you need within you." I woke up in tears. That's the message I needed to hear to remove the anxiety of finding a teacher. I began a regular meditation practice immediately. I turned the dogs' room, that they didn't use anymore, into my meditation room. It later became the healing room in which I'd give client energy healing sessions. I was already a ferocious reader, but I redirected my reading toward spiritual beliefs and practices from around the world. It was almost a year into my journey that I found a teacher to support my spiritual awakening.

ARE THEY THE ONE FOR YOU?

When you decide the time is right to find a human teacher, coach, or mentor, there are a few things to keep in mind. First, you want to understand their training. There are a lot of spiritual teachers, life coaches, and mentors out there, but not all of them will know or understand your experience or how to support you. There is no doubt that they will do their best and have only positive intent. But suggesting tools or techniques when they don't understand what you've been through can do more damage than healing. Traditional coaches and mentors are usually goal-oriented, focused on creating action plans and timelines. In my experience, these don't work for spiritual awakening and cause more frustration, stress, and anxiety. There are also some coaches and mentors who claim to "be woke" but are still stuck in ego, focused on material things, status, and external matters instead of internal, soul matters. Take your time to get to know prospective teachers, coaches, or mentors. Find the right fit for you, not the one that has the best sales pitch.

For example, I have both traditional and non-traditional backgrounds and training, and I'm a little "woo-woo." I have two life coaching certifications because I wanted both a "traditional" coaching training and one rooted in the spiritual awakening process. My Whole Person Coaching Certification is from Coach Training World. This is an International Coaching Federation (ICF) accredited coach training program focused on the whole person – mind, body, heart, and spirit. It is rooted in interpersonal neuro-biology, mindfulness, and somatics, as well as narrative and archetypal psychology. My Deep Transformational Coaching Certification from the Center for Transformational Coaching and Living is an ICF accredited program grounded in practical psychology, spiritual wisdom, and consciousness studies. My Deep Coaching training gave me powerful frameworks, skills, language, and practices to facilitate profound inner change within others and the communities and organizations in which they live and work. I'm also a Reiki Master, trained in sound healing, I continue my studies in Shamanic healing and journeying practices, Human Design, and intuition development. I continue to expand my knowledge and skills through additional course-work, classes, books, and continued training. My training is specific to the spiritual awakening process because I didn't want anyone else to feel the way I did. I've been through the spiritual awakening process, adjusting to life afterwards, and I am very dedicated to my continued development and transformation.

Understanding the basis for my training and beliefs may make me, or someone like me, a great fit for you. Maybe you love the idea of combining transformational coaching from a former business leader with alternative healing like Reiki, meditation, and intuitive readings into a program to help you on your own journey. Maybe someone with my background and beliefs is a little too "different" for you and you need someone that is more analytical and linear in their support and guidance. Get to know the background, training, and beliefs of the people you want to invest in before you make the investment so you get the most out of the relationship.

FRIENDS IN LOW AND HIGH PLACES

We've talked a lot about how friends and family may not resonate with you. Finding your new people is so important. People you can talk to, share your experiences with, share your frustrations with, people you just want to hang out with that get you. People you want to invite to participate in the things that bring you joy (see your joy inventory list). People you can share the new you without fear of judgment or rejection. I call these people your soul family. The people who "see" you, who love, respect, support, and honor who you truly are without expectation of you being someone you are not.

Finding new friends as an adult is hard. Most adults are into their routines. They have their work friends, their non-work friends, and their family. I've even heard adults say things like, "I have enough friends, I don't need anymore." Talk about a warm welcome. Think back to the last time you made a new friend. When was that? How did you meet? How did you first hang out? How did you become friends? Did it feel awkward or comfortable?

Let's start with the type of people you want to meet. Look back over your joy inventory list. Start to identify things that you'd like to explore and do that have group settings and give you the opportunity to meet new people. This could be a class or workshop on a topic you are interested in. Perhaps you want to take an art or sculpting class. Maybe you are interested in a meditation class or one or more of the eight limbs of yoga. It could be an outdoor activity like hiking, cycling, kayaking, bird watching, or gardening, just to name a few options. Start with selecting your top three that you'd like to explore first. Then look for group activities in your area that fit your top three. Eventbrite.com, Meetup.com, or simply Googling "painting classes near me" are great ways to find and sign up for experiences aligned with your joy inventory list that also put you with groups on new people. Isn't it weird that "Googling" is a verb now? Anyway. Moving on.

You will naturally gravitate toward solitude after your spiritual awakening. If you are an introvert like me, this can become a huge challenge for meeting new people. Signing up for the event is the easy part. But going to the event is the first hurdle, followed by putting yourself out there as the second. I encourage you to go in with an open mind, an open heart, curiosity, compassion, and to give yourself permission to be okay with whatever happens.

I'M DIPPING MY TOES IN

Marie was new to town and she didn't know anyone. She moved to this area because she felt like it resonated with who she was. She wanted to slow down, get out of the rat race, connect with nature and her spirit more. She loved her solitude. All she felt she needed was her dog and the woods. But she soon realized she was lonely. She reached out to me for a reading to get clarity and guidance about what was next for her.

The cards told her what she needed to know. It was time to find her soul family. To put herself out there. The world was her oyster and there was so much beauty, freedom, and joy ahead of her. Energetically, I could feel her anxiety, the wall around her heart, and this fierce need to protect herself. She'd been burned badly by friends, family, and partners in the past. It was one of the reasons she learned to be so self-reliant. I encouraged her to find three upcoming events focused on things that she was interested in learning more about or exploring.

A week later I got a message from her that said, "I'm dipping my toes in." She had signed up for a pop-up sound bath, yoga in the park, and an online intuition development class. In the coming weeks, she attended the events despite her ego telling her not to go. She said she could feel her ego throwing a tantrum. Such a great visual. The sound bath was two hours and followed with tea and conversation. Marie bolted out of there after the sound bath, not participating in the tea and conversation. That was enough group interaction for her for one day. She enjoyed yoga in the park and started going weekly. She started to say "hi" and "how was your week" to people she started seeing weekly, and that energetically resonated with her. The online intuition development class became her people. She clicked with a few of the people in the class and they now connect weekly outside of the group to catch up, share experiences, and support each other in their day to day lives.

QUALITY OVER QUANTITY

Many people are told that a sign of success or being a good person is the number of friends we have. I strongly disagree with this. I think it is about quality, not quantity. It is better to have one or a few friends that we can be completely open, honest, and raw with than ten that we engage in superficial conversation with. That doesn't mean that every conversation needs to be deep and profound. But we need to have the people around that fully embrace all that we are and are also willing to lovingly call us out when we aren't in alignment with ourselves.

A common coaching tool is the values identification exercise. The values identification exercise is a self-assessment tool that helps you get clear about what values you prioritize and how they relate to your personal and professional lives and your overall happiness. Values are part of your inner compass to help you navigate life. This exercise will help you get clear on the values that you want to embody, and it can be used to understand the values that you want in your personal and professional lives.

Below is a list of values to help you get started. Pick the top ten that you embody. Then prioritize them for yourself. Repeat this exercise for the top ten prioritized values you'd like to see in your friends. If you feel so inspired, do the same for your career. These will become the guiding principles for who you want to surround yourself with. Give yourself permission to change these when you feel your values have changed. It is okay to change your mind as your needs change and you continue to grow and evolve.

VALUES LIST

This is not an all-inclusive list. Feel free to add or use the values that speak to you:

- Accomplishment/Success
- Accountability
- Adventure
- Beauty
- Calm, quietude, peace
- Challenge
- Cleanliness, orderliness
- Collaboration
- Commitment
- Communication
- Compassion
- Competence
- Creativity
- Decisiveness
- Discipline
- Efficiency
- Equality
- Excellence

- Fairness
- Faith
- Family
- Freedom
- Friendship
- Fun
- Generosity
- Gratitude
- Hard work
- Harmony
- Honesty
- Independence
- Inner peace, calm, quietude
- Innovation
- Integrity
- Joy
- Knowledge/Wisdom
- Love
- Loyalty
- Openness
- Peace
- Personal Growth
- Positive attitude
- Privacy
- Prosperity, Wealth
- Purpose
- Resourcefulness
- Respect for others
- Romance

- Safety
- Self-reliance
- Service (to others, society)
- Spirit in life (using)
- Stability
- Status
- Strength
- Timeliness
- Tolerance
- Tradition
- Trust
- Variety

PUTTING IT ALL TOGETHER

Understanding your top values will help guide the types of teachers, mentors, coaches, or friends that you want to be part of your journey. Remember that these are guidelines, not hard and fast rules. Finding your soul family to support you as you adjust to life after a spiritual awakening is incredibly helpful for navigating the road ahead. Having people to share your experiences with makes the journey much more fun too.

Time to break out your journal again. This time, I want you to brainstorm places you want to explore to find your soul family. Look up local events, virtual or in person, and start jotting down those that you want to attend. Once you have a list that feels complete, pick one to sign up for. This will be uncomfortable for many people. But as I said before, you have to get uncomfortable to grow.

LET'S CELEBRATE

You've been doing a lot of deep and powerful work throughout this book. If you haven't already, I want you to take some time today or tomorrow to celebrate how far you've come. We've worked through your old beliefs and behaviors, you've done a lot of healing and created the space for new beliefs, behaviors, and things that truly bring you fulfillment and joy. You've worked through resistance, reconnected with your intuition, and you have a plan for starting to find your soul family. Well done. Now do something to thank yourself for all of your work. Do something that feels decadent. Maybe that's a trip to the spa, dinner at a special place, signing up for that workshop you've been eyeing, or buying yourself that thing you've wanted for a long time. Whatever will make you feel extra special, do that. You deserve it.

GROWING FORWARD

"Remember that this is not something we do just once or twice. Interrupting our destructive habits and awakening our heart is the work of a lifetime."

— PEMA CHODRON

Spiritual awakening is a lifelong unfolding. It is just the beginning for the ever-evolving life that is ahead of you. Spiritual awakening isn't for the faint of heart, but you wouldn't be going through it if you weren't up to the challenge. There will be moments of growth, comfort, discomfort, frustration, confusion, lows, and then clarity, lightness, freedom, peace, joy, contentment, and the cycle will continue over and over again like the spiral of healing. I don't say this to make you feel defeated or fearful of the road ahead. I say it to prepare you for the road ahead. To help you get comfortable with the in-between. Who you are today is different than yesterday and will be different than who you are tomorrow. And that is perfect just as it is. You are perfect just as you are. You are worthy of love because you are love. You are part of the Divine, not separate from it. Remember that.

Being flexible, open, and curious about the road ahead will help reduce the amount of anxiety, frustration, and suffering, though I know that is easier said than done. You have several tools to use and practice when you start to feel stuck. You can create your own or find other tools and practices that work for you. There is no one-size-fits-all roadmap, so give yourself permission to explore and not be like anyone else.

There is a common phenomenon of "going low before you grow." I see this in myself, with clients, and with my soul family. There is a buildup of fear, anxiety, depressive thoughts, and feelings that precede a spiritual growth spurt. You may want to seclude yourself and "cave up" during these times. Give yourself permission to do what you need to do. Use grounding practices to connect with nature and practice a lot of self-care during these low times. Be kind, gentle, and loving to yourself through these lows.

Remember the mantra that Steve adopted to alleviate the physical manifestation of his suffering?

Adopt a mantra. Use your words to create a mantra that puts you in a place of allowing, acceptance, and trust. I adapted a mantra from one of my favorite Oracle card decks, *Work Your Light* by Rebecca Campbell. I use, "I am open to surrendering to the creations that are wanting to be birthed through me. May I be of service for the highest and greatest good for others and myself in a way that delights my mind, body, and soul." I sometimes repeat this several times a day when I am feeling extra anxious.

As I've shared, you will get stuck from time to time and become anxious about the unknown future. We've been conditioned to push through, strive, build, do more to "fix" the discomfort. But now is the time to "do" less and "be" more. This is incredibly counterculture. Especially for those of us that have found success by achieving. Just remember that those achievements left you feeling empty and unfulfilled, or you wouldn't be here. When we force things, we end up increasing the resistance, reducing our connection to our Higher Self, our intuition, and to Spirit. It can create more confusion and anxiety because you haven't "figured it out yet." Instead, practice being in the present moment.

PRESENT MOMENT

Staying in the present moment is your key to peace. As Eckhart Tolle shares in his book *The Power of Now*,

"The moment that judgment stops through acceptance of what it is, you are free of the mind. You have made room for love, for joy, for peace." Mindfulness practices are how you stay in the present moment.

There are hundreds, if not thousands, of books, classes, teachers, articles, videos, and the like about mindfulness. It became trendy not that long ago. But all of it is about being in the present moment and living intentionally. I'm going to share some of my favorite ways of staying in the present moment with you. I encourage you to explore others and find which ones are most effective for you.

Witnessing or becoming the observer is my favorite way to bring me back into the present. In the mornings, I go outside and put my bare feet in the grass. I intentionally notice how the grass feels on my feet. No judgment if it is good or bad. Simply that it is. The grass is wet, cool, and dark green. I then look to the south, where I'm fortunate enough to see beautiful Mount Rainer. I notice if the mountain is covered by clouds or not. If the sky is sunny or not. Noticing whatever I notice, free of judgment, expectations, or opinions. I turn to the east, the north, and the west, making observations of what is. Accepting what is, just as it is.

Breathwork is another great tool for bringing yourself back into the moment. You can use any one of the breathing exercises I shared in Chapter 7.

Intentional breathwork takes you out of your head and puts you into your body. It calms the nervous system and the mind, allowing you to feel more centered and balanced.

Dancing is a great way to move energy through your body. Any exercise works to get the energy moving through your body, but I especially like dancing. I often put on some random dance music and dance around my living room and kitchen when I'm feeling extra anxious. Within a few minutes I'm feeling less anxious and more joyful. Who doesn't love a spontaneous dance party?

The power of music and sound can't be underestimated in your spiritual growth journey and to help bring you into the here and now. I have alchemy crystal singing bowls, Himalayan singing bowls, bells, drums, and rattles. When my head is spinning or I'm trying to force a solution, I go into my healing room and pick up whatever is calling to me and play for a while. I have blasted through some big creative or problem-solving blocks while playing one of my instruments.

GUIDEPOSTS

Your emotions, physical ailments, thoughts, and diseases are your guideposts to understanding if you are acting in alignment with yourself or not. In Human Design, your type has a specific indicator if you are acting out of alignment, called "not self." As a Manifesting Generator, I feel anger and/or frustration when I'm not living in alignment. I also get migraines and my thoughts become consumed with petty issues that I would normally not even notice. These are my indicators that I'm doing something that isn't aligned with who I am and my values.

Tanya came to me for a Human Design reading. Human Design is the blueprint to your unique soul, purpose, and how you best operate in the world. She was also a Manifesting Generator and wanted to know if she was making the right career move. As I shared her chart with her, she understood that anger and frustration were signs for her that she wasn't in the right relationship, role, or that she wasn't spending her time on the things that were right for her. I helped her understand how to best use her energy and resources, how to listen to her inner guidance system, the best way for her to make decisions, and to understand that others don't operate or think like she does. I also gave her tools for working through her triggers and self-sabotaging behavior. Her chart also confirmed that the field she was pivoting to was much more aligned with her Human Design than the field she was leaving.

GRATITUDE

Getting wrapped up in the resistances, the lows, and the challenges is an easy trap to fall into. I've found that gratitude practices are a great way to remind you of how far you have come and all of the beauty and magic around you. I recommend you do this as a writing exercise because there is something magical about seeing it in front of you. Write down a list of everything you are grateful for. If it has been a while, capture everything from the past year.

First, start with yourself. What are you grateful for about yourself? What have you done that you are proud of? Are you grateful for your body that helps you move and allows you to support others? Maybe you are grateful for your ability to hold space for others in a way that allows them to open up to you and heal themselves. Perhaps you have become good at processing your triggers and learning from them. Maybe you are no longer wrapped up in the stories you used to tell yourself about other people because you now ask instead of assuming. Maybe you moved to a town or a place that resonates with you more than where you were. Did you take a class, read a book, or start a hobby that brings you joy? Write it all down.

Now, write down everything you are grateful for in your life – members of your soul family, your fur-baby, your mode of transportation, your home, your partner. Maybe you are grateful to live in a town that allows you to be who you are without fear. Perhaps you are simply grateful to have a pen and paper to write with. Write down everything that you are grateful for outside of yourself.

Read over your list. How does it make you feel? Sit with those feelings for at least a few minutes. Meditate on them if you'd like. I recommend you do this monthly to capture and remind yourself of all the things you are grateful for about yourself and everything in your life. You can also keep a gratitude journal or simply capture things that you are grateful for each day in your journal. I like to end my day thinking of three things that I'm thankful for. It helps end my day on a high.

HAVE FUN

Spiritual growth can feel like serious business. Fun is the first thing to go out the door because we feel like it is a luxury. It is our divine right to have fun. Life is meant to be enjoyed to the fullest. It helps us raise our vibration, reduces stress and anxiety, and helps us to stay more in the moment. Whatever fun is for you, whatever makes you feel like a kid again, makes you giggle and belly laugh – do more of that. Your Higher Self, your spirit guides, and the Divine all have a sense of a humor. They get bummed out when it gets lost on you because you are being too serious. They need to lower their vibration to connect with you, so meet them halfway by raising your vibration.

You may feel as if you don't know what fun is anymore, and that's okay. Start to explore with the curiosity of a child to discover what fun means to you now. Refer back to your joy inventory list to see if there are things on there that you want to do or try. Ask what people from your new soul family do to have fun, and be courageous enough to try those things. Be bold. Be daring. Give yourself permission to experiment with fun unencumbered.

In fact, I want you to make a deal with me now. I want you to promise me that you will have fun. This may seem silly, but I am dead serious. I want you to say out loud, right now, "Lyndsay, I promise I will infuse each day with fun and magic, allowing the mystery of the unknown to unfold in divine timing." I know you just read that, hoping I wouldn't notice. But I did. Say it out loud, please and thank you. Seriously. I'll wait.

YOU'VE GOT THIS

As you continue on your journey to adjusting to life after a spiritual awakening, to reconnecting with your true self, and creating an intentional life that is filled with joy and fulfillment, remember these tools, tips, and resources. There is so much power in connecting with the present moment to enjoy every ounce that life has to offer. Watch for and listen to your guideposts to let you know when you are living out of alignment with yourself. Practice gratitude to bring more joy and appreciation in your life. And above all, have fun.

11

THE STRUGGLE IS REAL

"Life is a series of natural and spontaneous changes. Don't resist them; that only creates sorrow. Let reality be reality. Let things flow naturally forward in whatever way they like."

— LAO TZU

Spiritual growth is the hardest work you will ever do. I discussed previously that it is easier to "help" other people than to work on yourself because you've experienced firsthand how hard it is to change yourself. We humans think it will be easier and more effective to change someone else or an external situation. That's what keeps you stuck in old patterns. That's what keeps you from connecting with your true self, living your purpose, or finding the freedom and peace you thought spiritual awakening promised.

You may have heard or read that once you go through a spiritual awakening, you are enlightened and free from suffering. The reality is that it is just the beginning. When people realize the depths that they need to go to, the work required to deprogram themselves, to understand why they do what they do or why they think what they think, to realize the people who used to be in their corner no longer understand them, it can just be too much. They don't reach out for help because they might feel helpless.

THE CONDITIONS

We are also taught that fulfillment comes from outside of us. We are taught at an early age that is comes from the life partner we choose, the money we make, the kids we have, the stuff we buy and collect, the vacations we take. We are advised to find teachers, experts, or go to others for advice because we can't possibly know what is best for ourselves. But as you now know, that isn't true. True joy, love, fulfillment, and peace can only come from within yourself. Only when you do the work to understand and integrate your shadow are you able to break free from the shackles of the programming that has kept you in a place of illusion.

Finding your new normal after spiritual awaking is hard because you are told you are broken or something is wrong with you if you don't assimilate to the societal norms. But you are not broken. Those around you can't understand why you aren't happy with the life you have. They don't understand why you don't share the same dreams, goals, and aspirations as the rest of society. To do more, to be more, to consume more. Therefore, your support system begins to wash away.

Adjusting to life after a spiritual awakening is full of challenges because you are connecting with emotions that you haven't experienced before. You probably don't have people in your life to demonstrate how to feel, process, and express these emotions in a healthy and productive way. Most people I know were taught to stuff their emotions. To compartmentalize them. It takes bravery to go sit with and explore the beauty in the depths within you.

It is hard because so many of us were taught that asking for help is a sign of weakness. We are left spinning in our own minds without the tools, resources, or people to help us understand what is happening to us or how to move forward. But it takes a strong, courageous person to recognize and ask for the help and support they need.

BREAK ON THROUGH TO THE OTHER SIDE

Finding your new normal after a spiritual awakening brings freedom, peace, fulfillment, and joy as you've never experienced. Imagine being able to be your authentic self without the worry of judgment, without worrying if you'll let someone down, without the worry of letting yourself down. Free from the voices that keep you stuck and small.

Imagine a life where you are in a state of flow. Not upset about what happened yesterday or worried about tomorrow. Moving with life with the ease and grace of water down a stream. Moving around, under, or over the stones and the branches trying to block you along the way. Moving through obstacles with little disturbance to your power.

Envision life knowing you have and are enough because you know the Divine will provide you with whatever you need. All you have to do it ask, be quiet enough to listen, and take inspired action when the Divine provides. And the Divine will provide. Be it through inspiration, introducing you to the right people to support you, giving you the resources you need at just the right time, or removing people, places, and things to make room for what the future holds for you.

See a life where you have access to all the guidance and clarity you need. By connecting with and tapping into your inner wisdom and intuition, you can make decisions and find solutions with ease. You only need to quiet the mind and connect with your body and your Higher Self to listen.

Picture a world where you are living your best life. You feel strong. Powerful. Unlimited and expansive. You feel connected to all life. You have great love and compassion for everyone and everything. You are fulfilling your purpose and your soul.

This is what you get to look forward to as you continue your work on your spiritual awakening journey. Use the tools you've learned, find your soul family, and find the right teacher, coach, or mentor to help you adjust to life after your spiritual awakening to celebrate and support you so you can become the person you were always meant to be and create the life you were always meant to live.

UNRECOGNIZABLE

I met Lana two years ago at a sound healing workshop. At the time, she was a sales executive, divorced with children, and had gone through her spiritual awakening. We talked at great length about her experience and mine. She was stressed and anxious about the future, but optimistic about what the future held for her. She had a plan to exit corporate and become a healer, something that resonated with her much more than her sales role. She, of course, was concerned with making enough money and what the people closest to her would think. She had been seeing an intuitive life coach and acupuncturist who warned Lana against making any drastic changes to her career because of the disruption to her lifestyle. She told Lana to keep her sales role so she could fund her training and business for the first year. But I could see that didn't resonate with Lana. She tried to stick to the plan she put together with this coach, but she became increasingly frustrated and unhappy. Then she took the leap. Lana left her sales job and went all-in on her business.

I saw Lana recently and she was almost unrecognizable. Yes, she looked the same, but her energy was completely different. She was less anxious and seemed much more at ease and in flow of whatever life brought her way. She had seen firsthand how the Divine supported her by bringing the opportunities and people in her life to help her along the way. She had a renewed sense of trust and felt more confident allowing life to happen for her. She reminded me, "Life is always happening for us, not to us, right?" She was radiant in her power.

12

A LIFE WELL-LIVED

"Following what nourishes your soul is the only way to go."

— LYNDSAY K. R. TOENSING

We have covered a lot of ground to help you adjust to life after your spiritual awakening so you can connect with your true self and create an intentional, well-lived life. I provided you with tools and practices to help you move forward with your new beliefs and make the changes you want, to create lasting change so you don't fall back into old habits, shared ways to find your soul family so you can surround yourself with the love and support you crave, and shared ways that you can navigate your spiritual growth ahead with confidence.

In Chapter 4, you learned about how your programming and conditioning created who you were and helped you explore who you are. Chapter 5 gave you tools for healing the past and helping you navigate things that come up as you adjust to your new life. You put together your joy inventory list in Chapter 6 so you can infuse your life with more fulfillment and joy. Chapter 7 gave you more tools for working through the resistance from others and yourself. You learned techniques for reconnecting with your inner wisdom and intuition in Chapter 8. Chapter 9 helped you understand the importance of your soul family and provided ideas for finding them. Lastly, Chapter 10 provided you with some insights into what to expect as you continue on your spiritual growth and transformation.

You now have several tools in your tool belt to help you navigate the continued learning and growth ahead of you. Tools to help you get to know and integrate your shadow. To understand what your ego needs so that you can move past the fear. To live a life that is bigger than your fear. Tools to help you understand the lessons your triggers and self-sabotaging behavior is trying to teach you. Tools to help you make changes to your thoughts, empowering you to create your reality. Remember that the only business you should be in is your own.

MY WHY

I wrote this book because I didn't have the support I wanted and felt I needed when I went through my spiritual awakening. I've been there. I've lived through the confusion, uncertainty, and fear. I've felt the pain, the sadness, the heartache, and the shame. I've felt the complete loneliness of not having anyone to talk to or understand what I was going through. No teacher, coach, or mentor to help me process all the changes in my beliefs, in my habits, in the ways that I wanted to show up and contribute to the world. I didn't find anyone that followed a traditional, societally acceptable path who later took an untraditional path. I wrote this book so you know that you don't have to do it alone. I want you to know that you are not abnormal for wanting to go against the grain of society and your programming. I want you to know that you can do it. You can become the person you were always meant to be. It will be hard, but that's why I'm here. That's why I wrote this book. To help you on your journey.

Paul H. Dunn said it best, "Happiness is a journey, not a destination; happiness is to be found along the way not at the end of the road, for then the journey is over and it's too late. The time for happiness is today not tomorrow." There will be ups and downs, trials, and tribulations along the way. But I hope this book gives you the tools and resources to make the journey a little easier, a little happier, and filled with love and joy along the way. May you listen to your intuition for guidance. May you have the patience and compassion when you take a step into a different direction that doesn't feel good. You tried. And that's what is important. May you have the courage to step into the fear and the unknown and be open to the endless possibilities and abundance that you are worthy of. Be patient when you don't see where the next step will take you, but trust that it is going to lead to something better.

That's the thing with this journey. We don't know the destination. We don't know where each step will take us. But the path becomes clearer with each step we take. So, take a step into the unknown. Follow what nourishes your soul. Allow for magic to unfold in the mystery ahead of you, and forgive yourself when you aren't feeling patient or compassionate. Forgive yourself when you feel yourself reaching for what is comfortable and easy. This is the hardest work you will do in your life. It is okay to slow down. Just don't stop. If you get stuck, remember the tools you've learned. Use the journal prompts. Meditate in a way that feels right for you. Reach out to your soul family. Reach out to your teacher, your coach, your mentor, or your therapist. Ask for guidance and clarity from your higher self, your angels, ancestors, your spirit guides, or the other light beings that support you on your path to your highest and greatest good. I call this team your high vibe spirit tribe. And then listen. Be open to how the messages come through to you. The lyrics in a song, a storyline in a movie, a billboard. Or maybe you get the messages directly via the clairs that we talked about. And then trust. The more you trust your high vibe spirit tribe, the stronger and clearer the messages will become.

MY WISH FOR YOU

I believe in a world where people are empowered to make the conscious choice to live a life of fulfillment and joy. We get this one life (that we remember) and it is our responsibility to ourselves and to our loved ones to live our best life. To be an example to others. It takes courage and boldness, and it helps to find people to support you along the way.

I hope this book helps you understand that there is nothing wrong with you. You are perfect as you are in this moment. There is no need to fight against what your soul is calling you forward to do because the Divine supports you. It will support your journey to your true self. Let go of the "shoulds, woulds, and ought tos." You have permission to follow your dreams. To let go of the things that no longer bring you happiness and joy. To say goodbye to the people, places, and things that aren't aligned with who you truly are so you can step forward to find what and who is aligned with you.

I hope this book helps you be more compassionate with yourself and your process. We have enough pressure in life to be a certain way. To be the best employee, sibling, partner, parent, etcetera. And we are the hardest on ourselves because of the expectations for perfection we've put on ourselves. Give yourself permission to let go of those expectations. Let go of the pressure to do, to perform, to be something that doesn't feel good. Give yourself permission to love yourself. To take care of yourself. To give yourself what you need right now.

I hope this book gave you the tools and wisdom to navigate your spiritual awakening journey, and the courage to ask for support when you need it. You have everything you need inside of you to adjust to life and find your true self after your spiritual awakening. But give yourself permission to ask for help, find a teacher, a coach, or a mentor that can help you overcome the challenges and obstacles faster. I truly hope you feel supported and surrounded by love and acceptance as you continue your path. I hope you feel more confident, excited, and optimistic about the magic and beauty of the unknown ahead.

MY REQUEST

I ask that, as you become more confident in navigating life after your spiritual awakening, you share your experience with others. Become an elder for the younger generations so they know they don't have to go through this alone. Normalize the experience for others. Make awakening, spirituality, healing, emotions, and asking for help part of everyday conversations. Embrace and nurture intuitive gifts. Your own and others'. The more that people talk about and share the wisdom, tools, and resources they gain along the way, the more we help humanity connect with their divine selves and live a life of purpose, fulfillment, peace, and joy.

ACKNOWLEDGMENTS

Life is funny. We try to control the world around us until we realize we have no control. And then we just try our best to move like the water down the rapids. Looking back on the journey reminds me of how far I've come, all of the signs along the way, all of the people who came into my life at just the right time to help me see my true self. It took a long time. I mean…a LONG time. But I am so grateful for each experience. Each lesson. And each person that I was blessed to know. There are no words that could fully represent the magnitude of the love and gratitude I have for the people who have helped me along my spiritual journey.

None of this would be possible, of course, without The Author Incubator team. Thanks to Angela Lauria, CEO and Founder of The Author Incubator, for believing in me and my message. Not once, but twice. To my developmental editor, Mehrina Asif, and managing editor, Cory Hott, thank you both for holding such beautiful space for my process and making this adventure seamless, easy, and oh-so-much fun. Many more thanks to everyone else at TAI, but especially Ramses Rodriguez for your magical TAI community coaching, KristaLyn Montrose and Cheyenne Giesecke for helping keep all of us organized and on track. And to the entire TAI and Quill community for your kinship, love, and support as we embrace our lives as authors and change-makers.

A big thank you to my parents and my siblings (biological and other) for keeping an open mind no matter how uncomfortable my journey has made you. Ha! You keep me grounded while I continue to evolve and reach for my highest and greatest good. I very much appreciate your visits out to my corner of the world and our late-night chats about life. I love you to the moon.

To my grams, I miss you both so much every day. But I know you are here, helping me from the other side. Thank you for your continued guidance. I love you.

My soulmate friend, Kelly. I don't know if I would have had the courage to explore the breadth of my curiosity had you not showed me every day that it was safe to do so. No matter how strange or fringe something seemed, you were right there cheering me on. You still are today. Thank you for showing me what unconditional love, support, and acceptance means.

As I began to expand my healing modalities, the Divine brought me you, Suchana. Meeting you at the Seattle Sound Temple's Art of Sound Healing workshop was divine intervention. You were the first person that I could talk to about my spiritual awakening journey. You were the first person I met who understood what I was going through. Our walking chats have meant more to my soul than I think I could ever express to you. And thanks for introducing me to India and the beautiful souls that traveled with us.

No shamanic workshop is complete without meeting at least one new member of your soul family. Shawna and Perry, you have been an essential part to my monthly ceremonies. Being part of the Owl Clan, sharing in magical drum circles and sound baths have been essential for my connection to community and the Divine. Thank you for welcoming me in with open arms and hearts.

To my soul sister, Brooke, on the other side of the world, thank you for being such a bright light and bringing joy and laughter to the sometimes heavy as hell work of spiritual awakening. Your friendship and mentorship have meant so much to me. I'm grateful that we can be in the same room through the magic of technology as often as we like.

To my dearest friend, Evan. Ferosha warned us that coaching our fellow students would turn us into friends. Ha! You have seen and supported me through my highest highs and my lowest lows. This last year would have been even more chaotic if I didn't have your coaching and friendship along the way. Thank you for reminding me of the power, beauty, and magic of our emotions, and making it safe to feel and express them.

To Tamara, thank you for giving me permission to give myself permission to embrace the fullest expression of myself. I hope you know how much your magic helps all of those around you. I'm looking forward to the day I get to hug you in person.

To Jess B, thank you for the gentle pushes to get uncomfortable with the spirit world and help me understand that I can connect with dead people. You are a force that is helping create a new Earth. Thank you for inviting me to be part of it.

To Robin, thank you for introducing me to Human Design and the incredible power and gifts that I've always had inside me. I'm always humbled by the amount of love and respect you give to all that you cross paths with. Your life, your path, and your work inspires me every day.

To all my teachers, formal and informal, thank you for walking the path before me and reaching back to help others on the way. For writing the books, creating the workshops, holding the ceremonies, and sharing your experiences and wisdom with the world. Thank you.

To Ben, my ride or die in this life. Thank you for always telling me to just keep being me. For encouraging me to stay on my path no matter if anyone else understood or not. For not expecting me to be anything other than my true self. I couldn't have asked for a better brother and friend.

And to my HB, what a ride, huh? You out of anyone have been stretched and made so extremely uncomfortable as we both continue to evolve and change. But at the end of the day, I feel how much you love, support, and accept me for who I am. No matter where this journey takes us, I hope I've made you feel the same. I love you madly.

Lyndsay Toensing is a certified transformational leadership coach, energy healer, intuitive medium, and author. She is passionate about empowering people on their spiritual journeys and helping them adjust to life after a spiritual awakening.

Lyndsay previously led business and consumer-integrated marketing and business strategy teams in medical device, health information technology, pharmacy benefit management, and eCommerce retail industries. She spent fifteen years leading teams, mentoring, and coaching businesses from startups to

Fortune 500 companies before starting her coaching and healing practice.

She has earned traditional and non-traditional degrees and certifications. Lyndsay earned her master of business administration with a focus in brand management from the University of Minnesota, Carlson School of Management. She earned her Whole Person Coaching® certification from Coach Training World and her Deep Transformational Coaching certification from Center for Transformational Coaching and Living. She is also a Reiki Master, a certified End of Life Specialist, a HeartMath Add Heart Facilitator™, and holds certificates in Sound Healing and Shamanic studies.

Lyndsay, a native Minnesotan, lives in the Greater Seattle, Washington, area with her partner and their fur-babies. She loves traveling the world to experience new cultures, world religions, and spiritual practices. When she's in Washington, she can be found at drum circles, at spiritual growth workshops, exploring new areas in the beautiful Pacific Northwest with her partner, snuggling up with the dogs by the fire, or watching a movie with her partner.

Website: https://LyndsayToensing.com/
Email: LyndsayToensingCoaching@gmail.com

ABOUT DIFFERENCE PRESS

Difference Press is the exclusive publishing arm of The Author Incubator, an educational company for entrepreneurs – including life coaches, healers, consultants, and community leaders – looking for a comprehensive solution to get their books written, published, and promoted. Its founder, Dr. Angela Lauria, has been bringing to life the literary ventures of hundreds of authors-in-transformation since 1994.

A boutique-style self-publishing service for clients of The Author Incubator, Difference Press boasts a fair and easy-to-understand profit structure, low-priced author copies, and author-friendly contract terms. Most importantly, all of our #incubatedauthors maintain ownership of their copyright at all times.

LET'S START A MOVEMENT WITH YOUR MESSAGE

In a market where hundreds of thousands of books are published every year and are never heard from again, The Author Incubator is different. Not only do all Difference Press books reach Amazon bestseller status, but all of our authors are actively changing lives and making a difference.

Since launching in 2013, we've served over 500 authors who came to us with an idea for a book and were able to write it and get it self-published in less than 6 months. In addition, more than 100 of those books were picked up by traditional publishers and are now available in bookstores. We do this by selecting the highest quality and highest potential applicants for our future programs.

Our program doesn't only teach you how to write a book – our team of coaches, developmental editors, copy editors, art directors, and marketing experts incubate you from having a book idea to being a published, bestselling author, ensuring that the book you create can actually make a difference in the world. Then we give you the training you need to use your book to make the difference in the world, or to create a business out of serving your readers.

ARE YOU READY TO MAKE A DIFFERENCE?

You've seen other people make a difference with a book. Now it's your turn. If you are ready to stop watching and start taking massive action, go to http://theauthorincubator.com/apply/.

"Yes, I'm ready!"

Thank you so much for reading *The Beautiful Unbecoming: The Ultimate Guide to Adjusting to Life after Spiritual Awakening.* If you've made it this far, I know you are committed to doing your work so you can create an intentional, fulfilling life after your spiritual awakening. Or you just skipped to the end. Either way, I'm happy you are here!

I would love to learn more about your journey as you adjust to life after your spiritual awakening. Please keep in touch (I'm most active on Facebook @lyndsaykrt and Instagram @ lyndsaykristinet), share your wins by emailing me at LyndsayToensing-Coaching@gmail.com, and visit LyndsayToensing.com for more resources, tips, and tools.